DIABETIC AIR FRYER COOKBOOK

110 FLAVORFUL, CRISPY, & HEALTHY RECIPES FROM BREAKFAST TO DINNER

TAMMY OWENS

Table of Contents

INTRODUCTION

Diabetes is a disorder that affects how your body utilizes sugar, most often glucose. When people with type 1 diabetes do not produce enough insulin, their bodies are unable to utilize glucose correctly. The condition also causes excessive blood sugar levels, making it difficult to manage urination or thirst. Diabetes, if left untreated, may cause heart, kidney, eye, and nerve damage. Diabetic ketoacidosis may occur when a person has too much sugar in their circulation.

The repercussions of untreated diabetes place a tremendous strain on persons who are unwell as well as those around them. As long as difficulties are discovered soon and treated appropriately, the result is considerably better for everybody concerned with the correct treatment.

Type 1 diabetes is a type of diabetes in which the body's immune system kills beta-cells in the pancreas. These cells generate insulin, which is required by the body to break down meals and provide energy to muscles, tissues, and cells. Type 2 diabetes is a type of diabetes in which your body either does not create enough insulin or does not utilize what it does make as well as it should. In both circumstances, you need more insulin than your body is capable of producing on its own.

Type 1 vs. Type 2 Diabetes

Diabetes type 1 is an autoimmune disorder. In type 1 diabetes, the immune system destroys pancreatic cells responsible for insulin synthesis. Although we don't know what causes this response, many specialists think it's caused by a gene defect or viral infection that creates the sickness.

Type 2 diabetes is a metabolic problem, but a new study reveals that it may also be an immunological disease. People who have type 2 diabetes have high insulin resistance or an inability to create adequate insulin. Many individuals have a genetic susceptibility to type 2 diabetes, which is exacerbated by obesity and other environmental causes, according to experts.

Diagnosis

Diabetes detection has gone a long way in the past several decades. Diabetes is now diagnosed using two basic tests: fasting plasma glucose (FPG) and hemoglobin A1C. The FPG test measures your blood sugar levels after an eight-hour fast to see if your body is digesting glucose at a safe pace.

The A1C test determines your blood sugar levels during the last three months. This is accomplished by measuring the quantity of glucose transported by your red blood cells' hemoglobin. Hemoglobin has a three-month lifetime, which enables us to examine it to know how long it has been transporting glucose and how much it has carried.

Diabetes Type 1 and 2 Symptoms

The list of symptoms in type 1 diabetes may be lengthy, including both significant and less visible clues. I've included the most frequent symptoms, as well as additional possible consequences, of type 1 diabetes below:

Excessive thirst: Excessive thirst is one of the less obvious symptoms of type 1 diabetes. It is caused by elevated blood sugar levels (hyperglycemia).

Frequent urination is caused by your kidneys failing to digest all of the glucose in your blood, forcing your body to flush away extra glucose via urine.

Fatigue is induced by the body's inability to metabolize glucose for energy in type 1 diabetes patients.

Excessive hunger: People with type 1 diabetes often experience persistent hunger and increased appetites. This is due to the body's acute need for glucose, despite its inability to digest it in the absence of insulin.

A vision that is cloudy or unclear: Rapid variations in blood sugar levels may cause vision that is cloudy or blurry. Untreated type 1 diabetes patients are unable to naturally manage their blood sugar levels, making rapid changes a regular occurrence.

Rapid weight loss: The most visible sign of type 1 diabetes is undoubtedly rapid weight loss. When your body runs out of glucose, it resorts to breaking down muscle and fat to survive. In type 1 diabetic patients, this may result in very rapid weight loss.

Ketoacidosis is a potentially fatal consequence of untreated type 1 diabetes. In reaction to a shortage of glucose being supplied to our muscles and organs, your body begins breaking down your fat and muscle into ketones, which may be used without the need for insulin. In typical concentrations, ketones are entirely safe. However, if your body is famished, it may end up flooding itself with ketones in an effort to sustain itself; the acidity of your blood that occurs as a result of this inflow of acid molecules may lead to more dangerous situations, such as a coma or death.

Type 2 diabetes symptoms often develop slowly and are modest at first. Some early indications of type 1 diabetes may include:

Excessive hunger: As with type 1 diabetes, those of us with type 2 diabetes will experience continual hunger. Again, this is caused by our body's need for fuel due to our inability to digest glucose.

Exhaustion and mental fog: Depending on the severity of the insulin deficit, type 2 patients may experience physical fatigue and mental fogginess throughout the day.

Another sign of type 1 and type 2 diabetes is frequent urination. Frequent urination is merely your body's effort to rid itself of the extra glucose.

Dry mouth and persistent thirst: It is unknown what causes dry mouth in diabetics; however, it is strongly connected to high blood sugar levels. Constant thirst is caused not just by a dry mouth but also by dehydration caused by frequent urination.

Itchy skin: Itching of the skin, particularly around the hands and feet, indicates polyneuropathy (diabetic nerve damage). Itching might be an indication of elevated levels of cytokines in your system, which can cause itching. Cytokines are signaling proteins and hormone regulators that are often produced in large numbers prior to nerve injury.

As type 2 diabetes continues and worsens, the symptoms may become very painful and deadly. Among the advanced signs are:

Slow healing of bruises, wounds, and abrasions: Many patients with type 2 diabetes have weakened immune systems owing to a lack of energy available to the body. In addition to a lack of energy, many people with diabetes have delayed circulation due to high blood glucose levels. Both of these characteristics contribute to a considerably longer healing process and increased infection risks.

Yeast infections are considerably more common in women with type 2 diabetes than in non-diabetic women. This is linked to increased blood sugar levels and a weakened immune system response.

Long-term high blood sugar levels may cause significant nerve damage in diabetic people. Neuropathy is thought to affect around 70% of persons with type 2 diabetes (Hoskins, 2020). Diabetic neuropathy is characterized by numbness in the extremities, particularly around the feet and fingers.

Dark skin patches (acanthosis nigricans): Some persons with type 2 diabetes may have much above normal amounts of insulin in their blood because their bodies cannot use it due to insulin resistance. This increase in insulin in the circulation might cause certain skin cells to reproduce and develop black spots on the skin.

Foods to Consume

Vegetables

Fresh veggies are never harmful to anybody. Adding vegetable-rich meals is, therefore, the best chance for all diabetes people. However, not all veggies have the same number of macronutrients. Some veggies are rich in carbs and hence unsuitable for a diabetic diet. We need to eat veggies that are low in carbs.

- Cauliflower
- Spinach with tomatoes
- Broccoli with Lemons
- Artichoke
- Garlic
- Asparagus
- Onions
- Ginger, for example.

Meat

Meat is not on the diabetic diet's red list. It is OK for diabetic individuals to consume meat on occasion. Certain forms of meat, however, are superior to others. Red meat, for example, is not a good choice for such folks. They should eat more white meat, whether it's fish or fowl.

The following are some healthy meat alternatives:

All fish, including salmon, halibut, trout, cod, sardines, etc. Scallops, mussels, shrimp, oysters, and so forth.

Fruits

Not all fruits are beneficial to people with diabetes. To determine if the fruit is good for this diet, take note of its sugar level. Some fruits contain a lot of sugar in the form of sucrose and fructose, which should be avoided.

Here is a list of popular fruits that may be consumed on a diabetic diet:

Nectarines Peaches Avocados Berries and apples Grapefruit, Kiwi, and Bananas Cherries Orange grapes Pears Plums Strawberries

Seeds and Nuts

Nuts and seeds are among the most nutrient-dense foods, with a diverse array of macronutrients that can never be harmful. As a result, people with diabetes may include nuts and seeds in their diet without concern for a glucose surge.

Pistachios, Seeds of sunflower Walnuts, Peanuts, Pecans, Cauliflower seeds, Almonds Sesame seeds, for example.

Grains

Diabetic individuals should be cautious while selecting grains for their diet. The goal is to use the least quantity of starch feasible. That is why no white rice is on the list; instead, more fibrous brown rice is used.

Multigrain, Whole grains, Brown rice, Millet, Barley, Sorghum, Tapioca

Fats

Fat consumption is the most contentious subject in the diabetic diet since there are diets high in fat that have been shown to be useful for diabetes patients. The lack of carbs is crucial. In every other case, fats are just as bad for people with diabetes as they are for everyone else. It is preferable to consume unsaturated fats.

Other vegetable oils, sesame oil, olive oil, canola oil, and grapeseed oil are fats derived from plants.

Diary

Any dairy product that induces a glucose spike in the blood, whether directly or indirectly, should be avoided on this diet. Aside from that, all goods are safe to use. Among them are the following:

- Milk that has been skimmed
- Cheese with a low-fat content
- Eggs
- Yogurt
- margarine or butter with no trans fats

Sugar Substitutes

Because regular sugars and sweeteners are absolutely prohibited on a diabetic diet, there are fake variations that may provide sweetness without increasing the number of carbs in the meal. These alternatives are as follows:

- Stevia
- Xylitol
- Natvia
- Swerve
- The monk fruit Erythritol

Make careful to replace them with caution. Because the sweetness of each sweetener differs from that of table sugar, use them in proportion to the strength of their taste. Stevia is the sweetest of the bunch; therefore, it should be taken with caution. A teaspoon of stevia may replace 1 cup of sugar. In terms of sweetness intensity, all other sweeteners are equivalent to sugar.

Foods You Should Avoid

Knowing a basic diet plan is beneficial, but it is equally necessary to be well acquainted with the products that must be avoided. With this list, you can completely eliminate sugar from your diet. There are several additional foods that, like sweets, may be harmful to a diabetic patient. So, let us go through them in more depth here.

Sugars

A diabetic diet should avoid sugar at all costs. When you become diabetic, you must say goodbye to any natural sweeteners that are high in carbs. They include polysaccharides, which easily break down into glucose once they enter our systems. In addition to table sugar, additional ingredients such as honey and molasses should be avoided.

- granulated sugar
- The brown sugar
- Sugar used in confectionery
- Molasses made with honey
- Sugar, granulated

Your mind and body will resist the dramatic shift. It is advised to make incremental changes. It means gradually replacing it with low-carb alternatives, day by day.

Dairy Products with a High Fat Content

Diabetes makes you more vulnerable to a variety of other serious conditions, including cardiovascular disease. As a result, specialists strongly advise avoiding high-fat foods, particularly dairy products. A high fat intake might make your body insulin resistant. So, even if you take insulin, it will be useless since your body will not utilize it.

Animal Saturated Fats

Saturated animal fats are bad for everyone, diabetic or not. As a result, you should avoid utilizing them in general. When preparing beef, aim to remove as much fat as possible. These saturated fats should be avoided in cooking oils. Keep any animal-origin fats to a minimum.

Vegetables with a High Carbohydrate Content

As previously stated, veggies high in starch are not ideal for people with diabetes. These vegetables may raise the carbohydrate content of meals. So leave them out of the dishes and enjoy the rest of the less starchy veggies instead. The following are some examples of high-carb vegetables:

- Potatoes
- Yummy sweet potatoes
- Yams, for example.

Ingredients High in Cholesterol

Bad cholesterol, also known as high-density lipoprotein, has the propensity to deposit in various body regions. That is why foods rich in bad cholesterol are hazardous for diabetes.

These goods should be substituted with low-cholesterol alternatives.

Products with a High Sodium Content

Sodium has been linked to hypertension and high blood pressure. Because diabetes is already the consequence of a hormonal imbalance in the body, the presence of excess sodium—another imbalance—may cause a fluid imbalance, which a diabetic body cannot handle. It adds to the disease's previously existing problems. As a result, avoid utilizing foods rich in salt. Store-bought products, processed meals, and salt all contain sodium and should be avoided. Use only "Unsalted" food goods, such as butter, margarine, almonds, and other stuff.

Sugary Beverages

Sugar is abundant in cola drinks and other comparable liquids. If you've seen the many video presentations that demonstrate the number of sugars in a single bottle of soda, you'd understand how harmful they are for diabetes individuals. Within 30 minutes of consumption, they may significantly raise blood glucose levels. Fortunately, there are numerous sugar-free versions of beverages available that are safe for diabetes individuals.

Sugar Syrups and Dessert Toppings

A variety of commercially available syrups are composed entirely of sugar. One example is maple syrup. For a diabetic diet, the patient should avoid such sugary syrups as well as the sugary toppings available in supermarkets. If you must use them, trust yourself and make them at home using a sugar-free recipe.

Candies and chocolates

Sugar-free chocolates or sweets are the greatest options for diabetics. Other processed chocolate bars and chocolates are exceedingly harmful to their health and should be avoided at all costs. You may experiment with sugar-free recipes to make healthy snacks and sweets at home.

Alcohol

Alcohol has the ability to slow our metabolism and suppress our hunger, which may put a diabetic patient in a life-threatening situation. A very tiny quantity of alcohol cannot damage the patient, but frequent or persistent use of alcohol is detrimental to health and glucose levels.

The Advantages of Using an Air Fryer

Many studies have shown that fried meals are harmful to one's health and well-being. However, the cooking procedure of an air fryer encourages a healthy approach to frying food without sacrificing flavor or crunchiness. As a result, air fryers are ideal for health-conscious people and diabetics. Why is this so?

The major reason behind this assertion is that air fryers use less oil while frying meals, which may save up to 80% more fat than deep fryers. Isn't that massive? Furthermore, the fried dishes in it have the same flavor and texture as ordinary deep-fried foods.

Furthermore, research has shown that eating too many fried meals increases the likelihood of adult obesity. The more fried food you eat, the more likely you are to acquire diabetes. However, frequent consumption of fried meals might jeopardize your health if you have type 2 diabetes. Thus, if you want to reduce your fat consumption and/or lose weight without reducing your fried food intake, you could convert to air-fried frying.

The fat content of an air fryer is reduced, which significantly decreases the quantity of calories. Deep-fried chicken wings, for example, are particularly greasy, but air-fried chicken wings have less fat and more protein.

Less fat and calories with maintained nutrients and components are beneficial to health enthusiasts, weight watchers, and diabetics. Foods made in a deep fryer contain more calories and fats than those prepared in an air fryer. These fats and calories are also much too excessive to be a part of a healthy diet. As a result, consuming low-fat meals made in an air fryer benefits your health. As a consequence, the chances of health disorders such as obesity, heart disease, heart attack, blocked arteries, internal inflammation, and others will be reduced.

With this knowledge, you can see how the air fryer may help anybody who is attempting to manage or avoid diabetes and eat healthily.

Air Fryer Basics

To get the most out of your air fryer, you should look to buy the right air fryer for your individual needs. The type of cooking and baking you plan to use the air fryer for, the number of people you will be cooking for, and the amount of cooking you will do in your air fryer will all contribute to the air fryer model you should buy.

I have put together this detailed guide for you to make sure you purchase the right air fryer and get tarted safely and correctly with your new cooking ventures. Purchasing the wrong air fryer can cost you money if you realize you need a bigger size or if your machine breaks due to overuse of an underperforming model, so I have drawn up the best models currently on the market to help you make an informed decision and allowing you to get tarted on healthy eating instead of wasting time with empty promises from online sales ads. Firstly, you should know exactly why purchasing an air fryer is a great investment.

The Advantages of Air Fryers

Air fryers don't only offer a convenient and faster cooking method, they also reduce the levels of unhealthy fats in foods. Since you are looking at a healthy high-fat keto diet, you may wonder if this is counterproductive for your needs. It's not since you should be incorporating healthy fats into your diet and not deep-fried unhealthy foods. Air

fryers offer the perfect alternative to deep fryers by providing crispy foods with a lot less unhealthy oil being used. However, air fryers

are not only perfect for crisping up food, but they can also cook almost anything you would cook in a normal oven, including baked goods and treats. There are numerous benefits to using an air fryer:

Air Fryers Promote Weight Loss

A high intake of unhealthy fried foods is a common contributor to many health problems including heart disease, diabetes,

and cancer. Using an air fryer will help cut down on these fried foods by offering an alternative to deep-frying. You can enjoy the crunchy crispiness of battered foods while only using a small portion of the oil used in deep frying.

Air Fryers Reduce the Formation of Harmful Compounds

When cooking foods in large quantities of oil, it causes the food to heat up to extremely high temperatures. At these temperatures, a toxic chemical called acrylamide can form on the food (Link, 2018). This toxic compound has been linked to the possibility of causing various cancers, including ovarian, breast, endometrial, esophageal, and kidney cancer among others (Ryan, 2019).

Choosing a cooking method that removes the high oil content will help reduce the chances of acrylamides forming. Air fryers have been found to reduce the acrylamide content in potatoes by up to 90% (Sansano et al., 2015). The ketogenic diet also promotes the consumption of healthier fats rather than highly processed, unhealthy fats, so you can be sure that these recipes are limited to healthy oils in the cooking methods.

Air Fryers Produce Less Mess

Cooking with an air fryer reduces the number of oily dishes that accumulate in your sink after cooking and, in general, you will use fewer roasting dishes and trays since the air fryer has a built-in roasting basket. This reduces the amount of washing and prevents greasy dishes due to the reduction of oil in the cooking process.

Air Fryers Save You Time

f you prefer to spend less time in the kitchen and more time enjoying the food you cook, the air fryer offers you this opportunity by cutting down the cooking times. Since the airflow in the fryer moves faster around the food, you can enjoy cooking a lot quicker than using a large oven. With all these benefits in mind, there are also a few precautions to take into consideration.

Choosing the Right Air Fryer

There are many considerations to take into account when purchasing your air fryer, including the size, capacity, and functions. Once you have considered these, you should be able to choose the right air fryer for you.

The Size

Since air fryers have the great reputation of cooking fried food with a fraction of the oil, this may lead you to believe that you can now eat more fried food, since it is healthier now, right? Not exactly, because fried food is still fried food. The processed foods which come in frozen quantities such as French fries and other quick solutions to cooking are full of unhealthy ingredients that you will still be consuming even when frying them using less oil. t can be easy to

think that everything you put into the air fryer is now healthier but it is better to not fall into this trap. Luckily, this book omits the unhealthy fried food options and offers you 500 healthy alternatives that you will enjoy even more than fried foods. Plus, you get all the benefits of faster cooking times and healthier cooking with your air fryer.

The Capacity

Next, the inside of the air fryer is important. s there enough room to cook the amount of food you will be cooking? f you are only cooking for yourself, you may opt for a smaller model to work within your budget and to save on your energy bill. However, if you are cooking for a larger family, you should consider a bigger air fryer so you don t have to keep cooking in batches, since it will likely cost you more money on energy in the long run.

The Functions

Once you have chosen your size, are you looking for something with simple cooking functions, or would you like a more complex model that offers dehydration abilities or a toaster oven? You can also look for models with pre-programmed settings for the foods you will be cooking the most. You should also consider the temperature abilities of the air fryer. Make sure you choose a model that can heat up high enough if you will be cooking whole chickens and other meats.

FRY   BAKE   GRILL   ROAST

BREAKFAST

1. Breakfast Burrito

Prep Time: 7 min　　**Cooking Time:** 10 min　　**Servings:** 2

Ingredients

- 1 whole wheat tortilla
- 2 eggs
- 2 tbsp. of grated cheese
- 2 tbsp. of chopped bell peppers
- 2 tbsp. of chopped onions

Directions

1. Crack the eggs into a bowl and whisk together.
2. Add the grated cheese, bell peppers and onions to the bowl and mix together.
3. Place the tortilla onto a flat surface.
4. Spread the egg mixture onto the tortilla.
5. Roll up the tortilla and secure the ends.
6. Spray the air fryer basket with some cooking oil.
7. Place the burrito into the air fryer basket.
8. Set the temperature to **350°F** and cook for 10 minutes.
9. Serve the burrito with a side of your favorite salsa.

Nutrition: calories: 224, fat: 11g, protein: 12g, carbs: 20g

2. Tofu Scramble

Prep Time: 5 min　　**Cooking Time:** 18 min　　**Servings:** 3

Ingredients

- 12 ounces tofu, extra-firm, drained, ½-inch cubed
- 1 tsp. garlic powder
- 1 tsp. onion powder
- 1 tsp. paprika
- ½ tsp. ground black pepper
- ½ tsp. salt
- 1 tbsp. olive oil
- 2 tsp. xanthan gum

Directions

1. Switch on the air fryer, grease it with olive oil, then set the fryer at **220°F** and preheat for 5 minutes.
2. Meanwhile, place tofu pieces in a bowl, drizzle with oil, and sprinkle with xanthan gum and toss until well coated.
3. Add remaining ingredients to the tofu and then toss until well coated.
4. Open the fryer, add tofu in it, close with its lid and cook for 13 minutes until nicely golden and crispy, shaking the basket every 5 minutes.
5. When air fryer beeps, open its lid, transfer tofu onto a serving plate and serve.

Nutrition: calories: 94, carbs: 5g, fat: 5g, protein: 6g

2. Fried Egg

Ingredients

- 1 egg, pastured
- 1/8 tsp. salt
- 1/8 tsp. cracked black pepper

Prep Time: 5 min   **Cooking Time:** 4 min   **Servings:** 1

Directions

1. Take the fryer pan, grease it with olive oil and then crack the egg in it.
2. Switch on the air fryer, insert fryer pan, then shut with its lid, and set the fryer at **370ºF**.
3. Set the frying time to 3 minutes, then when the air fryer beeps, open its lid and check the egg; if egg needs more cooking, then air fryer it for another minute.
4. Transfer the egg to a serving plate, season with salt and black pepper and serve.

Nutrition: calories: 90, carbs: 0.6g, fat: 7g, protein: 6.3g, fiber: 0g

3. Scotch Eggs

Ingredients

- 1-pound pork sausage, pastured
- 2 tbsp. chopped parsley
- 1/8 tsp. salt
- 1/8 tsp. grated nutmeg
- 1 tbsp. chopped chives
- 1/8 tsp. ground black pepper
- 2 tsp. ground mustard, and more as needed
- 4 eggs, hard-boiled
- 1 cup shredded parmesan cheese, low-fat

Prep Time: 10 min   **Cooking Time:** 15 min   **Servings:** 4

Directions

1. Grease the air fryer pan with olive oil and set the fryer at **400ºF** and preheat for 10 minutes.
2. Meanwhile, place sausage in a bowl, add salt, black pepper, parsley, chives, nutmeg, and mustard, then stir until well mixed and shape the mixture into four patties.
3. Peel each boiled egg, then place an egg on a patty and shape the meat around it until the egg has evenly covered.
4. Place cheese in a shallow dish, and then roll the egg in the cheese until covered completely with cheese; prepare remaining eggs in the same manner.
5. Then open the fryer, add eggs in it, close with its lid and cook for 15 minutes at **400ºF** until nicely golden and crispy, turning the eggs and spraying with oil halfway through the frying.
6. When the air fryer beeps, open its lid, transfer eggs onto a serving plate and serve with mustard.

Nutrition: calories: 533, carbs: 2g, fat: 43g, protein: 33g, fiber: 1g

5. Spinach & Tomato Frittata

Ingredients

- 4 tbsp. chopped spinach
- 4 mushrooms, sliced
- 3 cherry tomatoes, halved
- 1 green onion, sliced
- 1 tbsp. chopped parsley
- ¾ tsp. salt
- 1 tbsp. chopped rosemary
- 4 eggs, pastured
- 3 tbsp. heavy cream, reduced-fat
- 4 tbsp. grated cheddar cheese, reduced-fat

Prep Time: 5 min **Cooking Time:** 21 min **Servings:** 4

Directions

1. Grease the air fryer pan with olive oil, then shut with its lid, set the fryer at **350°F** and preheat for 5 minutes.
2. Meanwhile, crack eggs in a bowl, whisk in the cream until smooth, then add remaining ingredients and stir until well combined.
3. Then open the fryer, pour the frittata mixture in it, close with its lid and cook for 12 to 16 minutes until its top is nicely golden, frittata has set, and inserted toothpick into the frittata slides out clean.
4. When air fryer beeps, open its lid, transfer frittata onto a serving plate, then cut into pieces and serve.

Nutrition: calories: 147, carbs: 3g, fat: 11g, protein: 9g, fiber: 1g

6. Herb Frittata

Ingredients

- 2 tbsp. chopped green scallions
- ½ tsp. ground black pepper
- 2 tbsp. chopped cilantro
- ½ tsp. salt
- 2 tbsp. chopped parsley
- ½ cup half and half, reduced-fat
- 4 eggs, pastured
- 1/3 cup shredded cheddar cheese, reduced-fat

Prep Time: 10 min **Cooking Time:** 25 min **Servings:** 4

Directions

1. Grease the air fryer pan with olive oil, then shut with its lid, set the fryer at **330°F** and preheat for 10 minutes.
2. Meanwhile, take a round heatproof pan that fits into the fryer basket, grease it well with oil and set aside until required.
3. Crack the eggs in a bowl, beat in half-and-half, then add remaining ingredients, beat until well mixed and pour the mixture into prepared pan.
4. Open the fryer, place the pan in it, close with its lid and cook for 15 minutes at **330°F** until its top is nicely golden, frittata has set and inserted toothpick into the frittata slides out clean.
5. When air fryer beeps, open its lid, take out the pan, then transfer frittata onto a serving plate, cut it into pieces and serve.

Nutrition: calories: 141, carbs: 2g, fat: 10g, protein: 8g, fiber: 0g

7. Chia Pie

Ingredients

- 1 cup almond flour
- 2 tbsp. chia seeds
- 4 eggs, beaten
- 4 tbsp. Erythritol
- 1 tsp. vanilla extract
- 2 tbsp. coconut oil, melted

Prep Time: 10 min   **Cooking Time:** 30 min   **Servings:** 8

Directions

1. Brush the air fryer basket with coconut oil.
2. Then mix almond flour with chia seeds, eggs, vanilla extract, and Erythritol.
3. Put the mixture in the air fryer basket, flatten it into the shape of the pie and cook at **365ºF** for 30 minutes.

Nutrition: calories: 134, fat: 10.9g, protein: 6.1g, carbs: 3.7g

8. Ricotta Muffins

Ingredients

- 4 tsp. ricotta cheese
- 1 egg, beaten
- ½ tsp. baking powder
- 1 tsp. vanilla extract
- 8 tsp. coconut flour
- 3 tbsp. coconut cream
- 2 tsp. Erythritol cooking spray

Prep Time: 15 min   **Cooking Time:** 11 min   **Servings:** 4

Directions

1. Spray the muffin molds with cooking spray.
2. Then mix all ingredients in the mixing bowl.
3. When you get a smooth batter, pour it in the muffin molds and place in the air fryer basket.
4. Cook the muffins at **365ºF** for 11 minutes.

Nutrition: calories: 75, carbs: 5g, fat: 4.6g, protein: 3.9g

9. Meatballs and Creamy Potatoes

Ingredients

- 12 oz. lean ground beef
- 1 medium onion, finely chopped
- 1 tbsp. Parsley leaves, finely chopped
- ½ tbsp. Fresh thyme leaves
- ½ tsp. minced garlic
- 2 tbsp olive oil
- 1 tsp. salt
- 1 tsp. ground black pepper
- 1 large egg
- 3 tbsp. bread crumbs
- 1 cup half & half, or ½ cup whole milk and
- ½ cup cream mixed
- 7 medium russet potatoes
- ½ tsp. ground nutmeg
- ½ c. grated gruyere cheese

Prep Time: 45-50 min   **Cooking Time:** 15 min   **Servings:** 4-6

Directions

1. Place the ground beef, onions, parsley, thyme, garlic, olive oil, salt and pepper, egg, and breadcrumbs in a bowl, and mix well.
2. Place in refrigerator until needed.
3. In another bowl, place half & half and nutmeg, and whisk to combine.
4. Peel and slice them 1/8 to 1/5 of an inch, if needed, to use a mandolin.
5. Warm up the Air Fryer to **390°F**.
6. Place potato slices in a bowl with half & half and toss to coat well.
7. Layer the potato slices in an Air Fryer baking accessory and pour over the leftover half & half.
8. Bake for 25 minutes at **390°F**. Shape mixture into inch and half balls.
9. When potatoes are cooked, place meatballs on top of them in one layer and cover with the grated Gruyere.
10. Cook for another 10 minutes. Enjoy!

Nutrition: calories: 232, fat: 8.2g, protein: 12.3g, carbs: 6.2g

10. Rhubarb Pie

Ingredients

- 4 oz rhubarb, chopped
- ¼ cup coconut cream
- 1 tsp. vanilla extract
- ¼ cup Erythritol
- 1 cup coconut flour
- 1 egg, beaten
- 4 tbsp. coconut oil, softened

Prep Time: 15 min   **Cooking Time:** 20 min   **Servings:** 6

Directions

1. Mix coconut cream with vanilla extract, Erythritol, coconut flour, egg, and coconut oil.
2. When the mixture is smooth, add rhubarb and stir gently.
3. Pour the mixture in the air fryer and cook the pie at **375°F** for 20 minutes.
4. Cool the cooked pie and cut into servings.

Nutrition: calories: 141, carbs: 5.9g, fat: 13.2g, protein: 2.4g

11. Lemon Pie

Ingredients

- 1 cup coconut flour
- ½ lemon, sliced
- ¼ cup heavy cream
- 2 eggs, beaten
- 2 tbsp. Erythritol
- 1 tsp. baking powder

Prep Time: 10 min   **Cooking Time:** 35 min   **Servings:** 6

Directions

1. Spray the air fryer basket with cooking spray.
2. Then line the bottom of the air fryer with lemon.
3. In the mixing bowl, mix coconut flour with heavy cream, eggs, Erythritol, and baking powder.
4. Pour the batter over the lemons and cook the pie at **365°F** for 35 minutes.

Nutrition: calories: 95, fat: 6.7g, protein: 3.7g, carbs: 5.4g

12. Bagels

Ingredients

- ½ lb. flour
- 1 tsp. active dry yeast
- ½ cup lukewarm water
- 2 tbsp. butter softened
- 1 tsp. salt
- 1 large egg

Prep Time: 20 min   **Cooking Time:** 15 min   **Servings:** 12

Directions

1. Liquefy the yeast in the warm water. Let rest for 5 minutes.
2. Add the remaining ingredients and mix until sticky dough forms. Cover and let rest for 40 minutes.
3. Massage the dough on a lightly floured surface and divide it into 5 large balls. Let rest for 4 minutes.
4. Preheat the air fryer to **360°F**.
5. Flatten the dough balls and make a hole in the center of each.
6. Arrange the bagels on a baking sheet lined with parchment paper — Bake for 20 minutes.
7. Enjoy!

Nutrition: calories: 232, carbs: 6.2g, fat: 8.2g, protein: 12.3g

13. Vegetarian Omelet

Ingredients

- 8 oz. spinach leaves
- 3 spring onions, cut into 1-inch slices
- ½ red bell pepper, cut into 1-inch cubes
- 1 cup button mushrooms, cut into ¼-inch slices
- ½ tsp. ground turmeric
- 1 tsp. thyme
- 1 tsp. Kala Namak salt
- ½ tsp. ground black pepper
- 1 tsp. minced garlic
- 3 tbsp. olive oil
- 2 tbsp. butter
- 1 cup chickpea flour
- 1 cup water

Prep Time: 16 min   **Cooking Time:** 15 min   **Servings:** 2

Directions

1. Place spring onions, bell peppers, mushrooms, turmeric, thyme, Kala Namak salt, ground black pepper, minced garlic, and 2 tablespoons of olive oil in a bowl. Toss well to combine.
2. Sauté for 3 minutes, frequently tossing.
3. Add spinach and butter to the pan, and sauté for another 3 minutes, frequently tossing.
4. Remove from the heat and set aside until needed.
5. Place the chickpea flour and water in a bowl and whisk to smooth the batter.
6. Grease the Air Fryer accessory with olive oil and pour in the batter.
7. Cook for 3 minutes at 390°F. Flip and cook for another 3 minutes.
8. Transfer fried Omelet to a serving plate and top with sautéed vegetables.
9. Serve with salsa on the side. Enjoy!

Nutrition: calories: 232, fat: 8.2g, protein: 12.3g, carbs: 6.2g

14. Sweet Baked Avocado

Ingredients

- 1 avocado, pitted, halved
- 2 tsp. Erythritol
- 1 tsp. vanilla extract
- 2 tsp. butter

Prep Time: 5 min   **Cooking Time:** 20 min   **Servings:** 2

Directions

1. Sprinkle the avocado halves with Erythritol, vanilla extract, and butter.
2. Put the avocado halves in the air fryer and cook at **350°F** for 20 minutes.

Nutrition: calories: 231, carbs: 2.9g, fat: 23.4g, protein: 2.2g

15. Sweet Potato Fritters

Ingredients

- (1) 15 oz. can of sweet potato puree
- ½ tsp. minced garlic
- ½ c. frozen spinach, thawed, finely chopped, and drained well
- 1 large leek, minced
- 1 flax egg
- ¼ c. almond flour
- ¼ tsp. sweet paprika flakes
- 1 tsp. Kosher salt
- ½ tsp. ground white pepper

Prep Time: 7 min   **Cooking Time:** 15 min   **Servings:** 4

Directions

1. Heat the Air Fryer to **330°F**.
2. Mix all ingredients.
3. Divide into 16 balls and flatten each to the only an-inch-thick patty.
4. Cook patties for 2 minutes at **330°F**.
5. Flip and cook for 2 more minutes.
6. If needed, cook in batches. Enjoy!

Nutrition: calories: 232, fat: 8.2g, protein: 12.3g, carbs: 6.2g

16. Hard-Boiled Eggs

Ingredients

- 6 pieces eggs

Prep Time: 2 min   **Cooking Time:** 10 min   **Servings:** 2

Directions

1. Arrange raw eggs on the rack of your air fryer, giving at least enough space to circulate the surrounding air.
2. Cook the eggs for 15 minutes in the fryer at **260°F**.
3. Remove the boiled eggs from the fryer and submerge them in a bowl with an ice-water bath for 10 minutes.
4. Peel the eggs and serve.

Nutrition: calories: 62, saturated fat: 1g, fat: 4g, protein: 5g,

cholesterol: 163mg, sodium: 62mg

17. Morning Mini Cheeseburger Sliders

Ingredients

- 1 lb. ground beef
- 6 slices cheddar cheese
- 6 dinner rolls
- Salt and black pepper, to taste

Prep Time: 10 min   **Cooking Time:** 10 min   **Servings:** 6

Directions

1. Preheat your air fryer to **390°F**. Form 6 beef patties, and season with salt and black pepper.
2. Add the burger patties to the cooking basket and cook them for 10 minutes.
3. Remove the burger patties from the air fryer, place the cheese on top of burgers, and return to the air fryer and cook for another minute.
4. Remove and put burgers on dinner rolls and serve warm.

Nutrition: calories: 261.7, fat: 9.2g, protein: 16.8g, carbs: 7.8g

18. Avocado and Blueberry Muffins

Ingredients

- 2 eggs
- 1 cup blueberries
- 2 cups almond flour
- 1 tsp. baking soda
- ⅛ tsp. salt
- 2 ripe avocados, peeled, pitted, mashed
- 2 tbsp. liquid Stevia
- 1 cup plain Greek yogurt
- 1 tsp. vanilla extract

For the streusel topping:

- 2 tbsp. Truvia sweetener
- 4 tbsp. butter, softened
- 4 tbsp. almond flour

Prep Time: 10 min   **Cooking Time:** 10 min   **Servings:** 12

Directions

1. Make the streusel topping by mixing Trivia, flour, and butter until you form a crumbly mixture.
2. Place it in the freezer for a while. Meanwhile, make the muffins by sifting together flour, baking powder, baking soda, and salt, and set aside.
3. Add avocados and liquid Stevia to a bowl and mix well. Adding in one egg at a time, continue to beat. Add the vanilla extract and yogurt and beat again.
4. Add in flour mixture a bit at a time and mix well. Add the blueberries into the mixture and gently fold them in.
5. Pour the batter into greased muffin cups, then add the mixture until they are half-full.
6. Sprinkle the streusel topping mixture on top of the muffin mixture and place muffin cups in the air fryer basket.
7. Bake in the preheated air fryer at **355°F** for 10 minutes.
8. Remove the muffin cups from the air fryer and allow them to cool. Cool completely, then serve.

Nutrition: calories: 202, carbs: 6.8g, fat: 8.7g, protein: 5.7g

19. Cheese Omelet

Ingredients

- 3 eggs
- 1 large yellow onion, diced
- 2 tbsp. cheddar cheese, shredded
- ½ tsp. soy sauce
- Salt and pepper, to taste
- Olive oil

Prep Time: 10 min   **Cooking Time:** 15 min   **Servings:** 2

Directions

1. In a container, whisk together eggs, soy sauce, pepper, and salt.
2. Spray with olive oil cooking spray a small pan that will fit inside of your air fryer.
3. Transfer onions to the pan and spread them around. Air fry onions for 7 minutes at **265°F**.
4. Pour the beaten egg mixture over the cooked onions and sprinkle the top with shredded cheese.
5. Take back into the air fryer and cook for 6 minutes more **265°F**.
6. Remove from the air fryer and serve omelet with toasted multigrain bread.

Nutrition: calories: 231.4, fat: 7.7g, protein: 12.8g, carbs: 5.7g

20. Cheese and Mushroom Frittata

Ingredients

- 4 cups button mushrooms, cut into ¼-inch slices
- 1 large red onion, cut into ¼-inch slices
- 2 tbsp. olive oil
- 1 tsp. garlic, minced
- 6 eggs
- Salt, to taste
- Ground black pepper, to taste
- 6 tbsp. feta cheese

Prep Time: 8-10 min   **Cooking Time:** 25 min   **Servings:** 4

Directions

1. Put the button mushrooms, onions, and garlic in a pan with a tbsp. of olive oil, and sauté over medium heat for 5 minutes.
2. Transfer to a kitchen towel to dry and cool.
3. Warm up the Air Fryer to **330°F**. Place eggs in a bowl and whisk lightly.
4. Flavor with salt and pepper, and then whisk well. Brush the baking accessory with olive oil.
5. Place sautéed onions and mushrooms in the baking accessory, crumble the feta cheese over it, and then pour the eggs on top.
6. Cook for 20 minutes and serve warm.

Nutrition: calories: 230, carbs: 5.8g, fat: 7.8g, protein: 11.8g

LUNCH

21. Chicken Wings with Curry

Ingredients

- 400 g. chicken wings
- 30 g. curry
- 1 tsp. chili
- 1 tsp. cayenne pepper
- 1 tsp. salt
- 1 lemon
- 1 tsp. basil
- 1 tsp. oregano
- 3 tsp. mustard
- 1 tsp. olive oil

Prep Time: 15 min   **Cooking Time:** 20 min   **Servings:** 4

Directions

1. Rub the wings with chili, curry, cayenne pepper, salt, basil, and oregano.
2. Put it in the bowl and mix it very carefully.
3. Leave the mixture at least for 10 minutes in the fridge.
4. Add mustard and sprinkle with chopped lemon on the chilled mixture. Stir the mixture gently again.   Spray the pan with olive oil and put the wings in it.
5. Preheat the Air Fryer oven to **356 °F** and put wings there.
10. Cook it for 20 minutes

Nutrition: calories: 244, fat: 10.6g, protein: 30.8g, carbs: 7.2g

22. Crunchy Brussels Sprouts

Ingredients

- 1 tsp. avocado oil
- ½ tsp. black pepper, ground
- ½ tsp. salt
- 10 oz. Brussels sprouts, halved
- ⅓ tsp. balsamic vinegar

Prep Time: 9 min   **Cooking Time:** 5 min   **Servings:** 2

Directions

1. Heat the air fryer at **350°F.**
2. Mix salt, pepper, and oil together in a bowl. Add the sprouts and toss.
3. Fry the Brussels sprouts in the air fryer for 5 minutes.

Nutrition: calories: 92, carbs: 12.1g, fat: 3.1g, protein: 5.2g

23. Crispy Fish Sticks

Ingredients

- 1 lb. whitefish such as cod
- ¼ C. mayonnaise
- 2 tbsp. Dijon mustard
- 2 tbsp. water
- 1 ½ C. pork rind
- ¾ tsp. Cajun seasoning
- Kosher salt and pepper to taste

Prep Time: 10 min   **Cooking Time:** 15 min   **Servings:** 4

Directions

1. Spray non-stick cooking spray to the air fryer rack.
2. Pat fish dry and cut into sticks
3. Stir together the mayo, mustard, and water in a small dish.
4. Mix the rinds and Cajun seasoning into another container.
5. Season.
6. Bake for 5 minutes at **350°F**, then turn the fish with tongs and bake for another 5 minutes. Serve.

Nutrition: calories: 253, fat: 16g, protein: 26.4g, carbs: 1g

24. Garlic Potatoes with Bacon

Ingredients

- 4 potatoes, peeled and cut into medium cubes
- 6 garlic cloves, minced
- 4 bacon slices, chopped
- 2 rosemary springs, chopped
- 1 tbsp. olive oil
- Salt and black pepper to the taste
- 2 eggs, whisked

Prep Time: 10 min   **Cooking Time:** 20 min   **Servings:** 2

Directions

1. In the air fryer pan, mix oil with potatoes, garlic, bacon, rosemary, salt, pepper, and eggs and whisk.
2. Cook potatoes at **400°F** for 20 minutes, divide everything between plates and serve for breakfast.

Nutrition: calories: 211, carbs: 8g, fat: 3g, protein: 5g

25. Garlic Rosemary Grilled Prawns

Ingredients

- ½ tbsp. butter, melted
- 2 green capsicum slices
- 8 prawns
- 2 Rosemary leaves
- Kosher salt and black pepper, freshly ground
- 3- 4 garlic cloves, minced

Prep Time: 5 min   **Cooking Time:** 10 min   **Servings:** 2

Directions

1. In a bowl, mix all the ingredients and marinate the prawns in it for at least 60 minutes or more
2. Add 2 prawns and 2 slices of capsicum on each skewer.
3. Preheat to **356°F**.
4. Cook for 5–6 minutes. Then change the temperature to **392°F** and cook for another minute.
5. Serve with lemon wedges.

Nutrition: calories: 194, fat: 10g, protein: 26g, carbs: 12g

26. Lemon and Pepper Aioli

Ingredients

- 4 Shishito pepper cut in half,
- 1 tsp. avocado oil,
- vegan mayonnaise (about a half cup),
- a couple of tablespoons of pure,
- unfiltered lemon juice,
- a single minced garlic clove,
- 1 tsp. of finely chopped fresh parsley
- A pinch of salt and a pinch of pepper

Prep Time: 15 min   **Cooking Time:** 8 min   **Servings:** 2

Directions

1. Vegan mayonnaise, freshly squeezed lemon juice, finely chopped fresh parsley, pepper, sea salt, and finely minced garlic should all be combined in a bowl and stirred until everything is evenly distributed.
2. Let it sit for a while so the flavors may mingle. Turn on the air fryer and let it heat up for about 3 min, until it reaches **380°F**.
3. Spread the shishito peppers out in a single layer in the air fryer basket after tossing them with oil. Broil for around 4 minutes in the air.
4. When done, the peppers will have developed tiny blisters and slightly softened.
5. Add 2 additional minutes of cooking time if it's still uncooked.
6. Remove the food from the basket, season it with salt and freshly squeezed lemon juice, and serve.

Nutrition: calories: 218, carbs: 5g, fat: 20g, protein: 1g, fiber: 2g, cholesterol 10mg

27. Bacon-Wrapped Asparagus

Ingredients

- Approximately 1 bunch of asparagus
- Bacon, 1 lb (regular sliced not thick)

Prep Time: 10 min   **Cooking Time:** 12 min   **Servings:** 8

Directions

1. Firstly, before using asparagus in the recipe, wash it and pat it dry with a dish towel, wrap a piece of bacon around each piece of tender asparagus; next, use a toothpick to secure the bacon-wrapped spears together.
2. Then cover the stems and bacon and cook them in an air fryer at **400°F** for about 12 minutes, or until the bacon is browned and the stems are firm.
3. Drain on paper towels and season with salt after they've been removed from the pan.

Nutrition: calories: 270, fat: 19g, protein: 18g, carbs: 1g

28. Zucchini Fries

Ingredients

- 2 zucchinis, medium size
- 1 large egg
- 13 cup almond flour
- ½ cup of grated parmesan
- ½ tsp. of Italian seasoning
- ½ tsp. garlic powder
- A pinch of salt
- A pinch of black pepper,
- ¼ tsp. of olive oil

Prep Time: 10 min   **Cooking Time:** 12 min   **Servings:** 4

Directions

1. First, cut the zucchini in half lengthwise, and then slice each half into many sticks that are about half an inch thick and four inches long.
2. Mix together the almond flour, Italian seasoning, grated parmesan, garlic powder, black pepper, and salt in a bowl.
3. Put the dish down, whisk the egg in a separate basin until it becomes foamy.
4. Dip the zucchini sticks in the egg, and then in the almond flour and salt mixture.
5. The zucchini sticks need to be sprayed with extra virgin olive oil spray, after coating the zucchini sticks with the seasoning, place them in the air fryer's basket and cook them for about ten minutes at **400°F**.

Nutrition: calories: 115, carbs: 6g, fat: 7g, protein: 8g, fiber: 1g

29. Jalapeño Poppers

Ingredients

- 6 medium jalapenos
- 4 ounces of melted cream cheese
- 6 to 12 slices of cooked bacon

Prep Time: 12 min   **Cooking Time:** 12 min   **Servings:** 6

Directions

1. The first step is to cut the jalapenos into halves of equal length. The jalapenos must have their seeds removed.
2. Wash the jalapenos thoroughly.
3. Second, slice the log of cream cheese into thin strips and stuff one piece into each pepper half.
4. Put the stuffed pepper on a baking sheet, stuff it with cheese, and then wrap it in bacon and secure it with a toothpick.
5. Cook the stuffed peppers in an air fryer by placing them in the appliance's basket.
6. Check for any potential overlap and eliminate it.
7. Put the food in the air fryer and cook it at **370°F** for about 12 minutes, or until it's as crisp as you like it.

Nutrition: calories: 80, fat: 7g, protein: 1g, carbs: 2g, fiber 1g

30. Low Carb Fried Pickles

Ingredients

- ¼ cup of grated Parmesan,
- 2 eggs,
- ½ cups of almond flour,
- 3 dill pickle slices
- a pinch of salt, optional.

Prep Time: 10 min   **Cooking Time:** 10 min   **Servings:** 4

Directions

1. Use cooking spray to coat the inside of the air fryer pan and the air fryer basket.
2. Put the two eggs in a bowl and put them aside.
3. Mix the ground almonds, salt, and parmesan cheese in a separate bowl.
4. After you have diced the pickles, you can roll them in the beaten eggs, after coating the pickles in the almond flour mixture, dredge them.
5. Arrange the slices of pickle in a single layer in the air fryer. Add the pan to the oven and cook for about five minutes at **360°F**.
6. After turning the pickle slices, continue cooking for another 5 minutes.

Nutrition: cholesterol: 84mg, carbs: 5g, fat: 10g, protein: 9g

31. Tuna Sandwiches

Ingredients

- 16 oz. tuna can and drained
- ¼ c. mayonnaise
- 2 tbsp. mustard
- 1 tbsp. lemon juice
- 2 green onions, chopped
- 3 English muffins, halved
- 3 tbsp. butter
- 3 provolone cheese

Prep Time: 10 min   **Cooking Time:** 5 min   **Servings:** 2

Directions

1. Mix tuna with mayo, lemon juice, mustard, and green onions in a bowl and stir.
2. Grease muffin halves with the butter, place them in the preheated air fryer and bake them at **350°F** for 4 minutes.
3. Spread tuna mix on muffin halves, top each with cheese, return sandwiches to the air fryer, cook them for 4 minutes, divide among plates, and serve breakfast right away.

Nutrition: calories: 182, fat: 4g, protein: 6g, carbs: 8g

32. Garlic Potatoes

Ingredients

- 4 potatoes, peeled and cut into medium cubes
- 6 garlic cloves, minced
- 2 rosemary springs, chopped
- 1 tbsp. olive oil
- Salt and black pepper to the taste
- 2 eggs whisked

Prep Time: 10 min   **Cooking Time:** 20 min   **Servings:** 2

Directions

1. Mix oil with potatoes, garlic, rosemary, salt, pepper, eggs, and whisk in the air fryer pan.
2. Cook potatoes at **400°F** for 20 minutes, divide everything between plates and serve for breakfast.

Nutrition: calories: 211, carbs: 8g, fat: 3g, protein: 5g

33. Shrimp Frittata

Ingredients

- 4 eggs
- ½ tsp. basil, dried
- Cooking spray
- Salt and black pepper to the taste
- ½ c. shrimp, cooked, peeled, deveined, and chopped
- ½ c. baby spinach, chopped
- ½ c. Monterey Jack cheese, grated

Prep Time: 10 min   **Cooking Time:** 15 min   **Servings:** 2

Directions

1. Mix eggs with salt, pepper, and basil and whisk. Grease your air fryer's pan with cooking spray, shrimp, and spinach.
2. Add eggs mix, sprinkle cheese all over and cook in your air fryer at **350°F** for 10 minutes.
3. Divide among plates and serve for breakfast.

Nutrition: calories: 162, fat: 6g, protein: 4g, carbs: 8g, fiber: 5g

34. Chicken Omelet

Ingredients

- 1 tsp. butter
- 1 small yellow onion, chopped
- ½ jalapeño pepper, seeded and chopped
- 3 eggs
- Salt and black pepper, ground, as required
- ¼ c. chicken, cooked and shredded

Prep Time: 10 min   **Cooking Time:** 16 min   **Servings:** 2

Directions

1. Melt butter and cook the onion for 4–5 minutes. Add the jalapeño pepper and cook for about 1 minute.
2. Set aside to cool.
3. Beat eggs, salt, and pepper.
4. Add the onion mixture and chicken and stir to combine. Place the chicken mixture into a small baking pan.
5. Cook 6 minutes at **355°F**.
6. Cut the omelet into 2 portions and serve hot.

Nutrition: calories: 153, carbs: 4g, fat: 9.1g, protein: 13.8g, fiber: 0.9g

35. Scrambled Eggs

Ingredients

- 4 large eggs
- ½ c. sharp cheese, shredded
- 2 tbsp. unsalted butter

Prep Time: 5 min   **Cooking Time:** 20 min   **Servings:** 2

Directions

1. Put eggs into a 2-cup round baking dish and whisk.
2. Place dish in fryer basket.
3. Stir the eggs and add butter and cheese.
4. Let cook for 3 at **265°F** more minutes and stir again.
5. Allow eggs to finish cooking for additional 2 minutes or remove if they are to your desired liking.

Nutrition: calories: 359, fat: 27.6g, protein: 19.5g, carbs: 1.1g

36. Mushroom Cheese Salad

Ingredients

- 10 mushrooms, halved
- 1 tbsp. fresh parsley, chopped
- 1 tbsp. olive oil
- 1 tbsp. mozzarella cheese, grated
- 1 tbsp. cheddar cheese, grated
- Salt and pepper to the taste

Prep Time: 10 min   **Cooking Time:** 15 min   **Servings:** 2

Directions

1. Mix all ingredients . Transfer mixture into the air fryer baking dish.
2. Cook at **380°F** for 15 minutes.
3. Serve.

Nutrition: calories: 90, carbs: 2g, fat: 7g, sugar: 1g

37. Tuna Sandwiches

Ingredients

- 16 oz. tuna, canned and drained
- ¼ C. mayonnaise
- 2 tbsp. mustard
- 1 tbsp. lemon juice
- 2 green onions, chopped
- 3 English muffins, halved
- 3 tbsp. butter
- 6 provolone cheese

Prep Time: 10 min   **Cooking Time:** 5 min   **Servings:** 2

Directions

1. In a bowl, mix tuna with mayo, lemon juice, mustard, and green onions and stir.
2. Grease muffin halves with the butter, place them in the preheated air fryer and bake them at **350°F** for 4 minutes.
3. Spread tuna mix on muffin halves, top each with cheese, return sandwiches to air fryer and cook them for 4 minutes, divide among plates and serve for breakfast right away.

Nutrition: calories: 182, fat: 4g, protein: 6g, carbs: 8g, fiber: 7g

38. Tex-Mex Salmon Stir-Fry

Ingredients

- 12 oz. salmon fillets, cut into 1½-inch cubes
- 1 red bell pepper, chopped
- 1 red onion, chopped
- 1 jalapeño pepper, minced
- ¼ C. low-sodium salsa
- 2 tbsp. low-sodium tomato juice
- 2 tsp. peanut oil or safflower oil
- 1 tsp. chili powder
- polenta, cooked

Prep Time: 15 min   **Cooking Time:** 9-14 min   **Servings:** 4

Directions

1. In an intermediate bowl, blend the salmon, red bell pepper, red onion, jalapeño, salsa, tomato juice, peanut oil, and chili powder.
2. Place the bowl in the Air Fryer and cook for 9–14 minutes at **350°F**, until the salmon is just cooked through and firm and the vegetables are crisp-tender, stirring once.
3. Serve instantly over hot cooked polenta, if desired.

Nutrition: calories: 116, carbs: 5g, fat: 3g, protein: 18g, sodium: 136mg

39. Zucchini Fritters

Ingredients

- 2 medium zucchinis, ends trimmed
- 3 tbsp. almond flour
- 1 tbsp. salt
- 1 tsp. garlic powder
- ¼ tsp. paprika
- ¼ tsp. black pepper, ground
- ¼ tsp. onion powder
- 1 egg, pastured

Prep Time: 20 min   **Cooking Time:** 12 min   **Servings:** 4

Directions

1. Wash and pat dry the zucchini, then cut its ends and grate the zucchini.
2. Place grated zucchini in a colander, sprinkle with salt and let it rest for 10 minutes.
3. Then, wrap zucchini in a kitchen cloth, squeeze moisture from it as much as possible, and place dried zucchini in another bowl.
4. Add remaining ingredients into the zucchini and then stir until mixed.
5. Take the fryer basket, line it with parchment paper, grease it with oil, drop zucchini mixture on it by a spoonful, about 1-inch apart, and then spray well with oil.
6. Cook the fritter for 12 minutes at **350°F** until nicely golden and cooked, flipping the fritters halfway through the frying. Serve straight away.

Nutrition: calories: 57, fat: 1g, protein: 3g, carbs: 8g

40. Chicken Nuggets with Sweet Potatoes

Ingredients

- 1 lb. of chicken ground
- 1 tsp. of onion powder
- 1 sweet potato
- 2 cup of whole-wheat crackers
- 1/4 cup oat flour
- 1/8 teaspoon of garlic powder
  Optional:
- ½ teaspoon salt

Prep Time: 20 min   **Cooking Time:** 16 min   **Servings:** 24

Directions

1. Create a coarse flour from the crackers. In a bowl, set aside. Cut the sweet potato into dice.
2. Combine the oat flour, ground chicken, and seasoning with the sweet potato dice. For these three stages, a food processor can be used. Use the mixture to coat the crushed crackers.
3. Make sure the coating is thick. Use paper to line the air fryer tray. Set the air fryer's temperature to **360°F**.
4. Use avocado oil to sparingly coat the air fryer tray to avoid sticking.
5. Place the coated chicken nuggets in the tray and drizzle extra avocado oil over the top.
6. Prepare the food for 16 minutes.

Nutrition: calories: 88, carbs: 9g, fat: 3g, protein: 4.2g, fiber: 1g

DINNER

41. Salmon with Maple Soy Glaze

Ingredients

- 3 tbsp. pure maple syrup
- 3 tbsp. gluten-free soy sauce
- 1 tbsp. sriracha hot sauce
- 1 garlic clove, minced
- 4 salmon fillets, skinless

Prep Time: 5 min   **Cooking Time:** 8 min   **Servings:** 4

Directions

1. In a bowl, maple syrup, garlic, and soy sauce with salmon.
2. Mix well and let it marinate for at least half an hour.
3. Preheat to **400°F** with oil spray the basket.
4. Take fish out from the marinade, pat dry.
5. Put the salmon in the air fryer, cook for 7–8 minutes, or longer.
6. In the meantime, in a saucepan, add the marinade, let it simmer until reduced to half.
7. Add glaze over salmon and serve.

Nutrition: calories: 292, fat: 11g, protein: 35g, carbs: 12g

42. Shrimp Scampi

Ingredients

- 4 cup raw shrimp
- 1 tbsp. lemon juice
- Fresh basil, chopped
- 2 tsp. red pepper flakes
- 2.5 tbsp. butter Chives, chopped
- 2 tbsp. chicken stock
- 1 tbsp. garlic, minced

Prep Time: 5 min   **Cooking Time:** 10 min   **Servings:** 2

Directions

1. Preheat with a metal pan to **330°F**.
2. In the hot pan, add garlic, red pepper flakes, and half of the butter. Let it cook for 2 minutes.
3. Add the butter, shrimp, chicken stock, minced garlic, chives, lemon juice, basil to the pan. Let it cook for 5 minutes. Bathe the shrimp in melted butter.
4. Remove from fryer and let it rest for 1 minute.
5. Add fresh basil leaves and chives and serve.

Nutrition: calories: 287, carbs: 7.5g, fat: 5.5g, protein: 18g

43. Beef with Mushrooms

Ingredients

- 300 g beef
- 150 g mushrooms
- 1 onion
- 1 tsp. olive oil
- 100 g vegetable broth
- 1 tsp. basil
- 1 tsp. chili
- 30 g tomato juice

Prep Time: 15 min   **Cooking Time:** 40 min   **Servings:** 4

Directions

1. For this recipe, you should take a solid piece of beef. Take the beef and pierce the meat with a knife.
2. Rub it with olive oil, basil, and chili, and lemon juice.
3. Chop the onion and mushrooms and pour them with vegetable broth. Cook the vegetables for 5 minutes.
4. Take a big tray and put the meat in it. Add vegetable broth to the tray too. It will make the meat juicy.
5. Preheat the air fryer oven to **356°F** and cook it for 35 minutes.

Nutrition: calories: 175, fat: 6.2g, protein: 24.9g, carbs: 4.4g

44. Beef Korma Curry

Ingredients

- 1 lb. (454 g.) sirloin steak, sliced
- ½ cup yogurt
- 1 tbsp. curry powder
- 1 tbsp. olive oil
- 1 onion, chopped
- 2 cloves garlic, minced
- 1 tomato, diced
- ½ cup frozen baby peas, thawed

Prep Time: 10 min   **Cooking Time:** 17-20 min   **Servings:** 4

Directions

1. Combine the steak, yogurt, and curry powder. Stir and set aside.
2. In a metal bowl, combine the olive oil, onion, and garlic.
3. Bake at **350°F** for 3 to 4 minutes or until crisp and tender.
4. Add the steak along with the yogurt and the diced tomato.
5. Bake for 12 to 13 minutes or until the steak is almost tender.
6. Stir in the peas and bake for 2 to 3 minutes or until hot.

Nutrition: calories: 299, carbs: 9g, fat: 11g, protein: 38g, fiber: 2g, sugar: 3g, sodium: 100mg

45. Classic Fried Pickles

Ingredients

- 1 egg, whisked
- 2 tbsp. buttermilk
- ½ cup breadcrumbs
- ¼ cup Romano cheese, grated
- ½ tsp. onion powder
- ½ tsp. garlic powder
- 1 ½ cups dill pickle chips, dry with towels

Mayo Sauce:

- ¼ cup mayonnaise
- ½ tbsp. mustard
- ½ tsp. molasses
- 1 tbsp. ketchup
- ¼ tsp. ground black pepper

Prep Time: 20 min   **Cooking Time:** 10 min   **Servings:** 2

Directions

1. In a narrow bowl, whisk the egg with buttermilk.
2. In another bowl, mix the breadcrumbs, cheese, onion powder, and garlic powder.
3. Dredge the pickle chips in the egg mixture, then, in the breadcrumb/cheese mixture.
4. Cook at **400°F** for 5 minutes; shake the basket and cook for 5 minutes more.
5. Meanwhile, mix all the sauce ingredients until well combined. Serve the fried pickles with the mayo sauce for dipping.

Nutrition: calories: 342, fat: 28.5g, protein: 9.1g, carbs: 12.5g

46. Zucchini Squash Mix

Ingredients

- 1 lb. zucchini, sliced
- 1 tbsp. parsley, chopped
- 1 yellow squash, halved, deseeded, and chopped
- 1 tbsp. olive oil
- Salt and pepper to the taste

Prep Time: 10 min   **Cooking Time:** 35 min   **Servings:** 2

Directions

7. Mix all ingredients. Transfer the bowl mixture into the air fryer basket and cook at **400°F** for 35 minutes.

Nutrition: calories: 49, carbs: 4g, fat: 3g, protein: 1.5g

47. Salmon Teriyaki

Ingredients

- 1/8 cup mirin (sweetened sake)
- ½ cup soy sauce low in sodium
- 2 garlic cloves minced
- 1/4 tsp of toasted sesame oil
- 1-inch gingerbread (minced) Salmon
- 1 1/2 pounds of skin-on salmon filets (cut into 4 equal sized pieces)

Prep Time: 10 min   **Cooking Time:** 6 min   **Servings:** 2

Directions

1. Place the prepared teriyaki sauce ingredients in a small saucepan and heat to a boil over medium-high heat.
2. Remove from burner after 5 minutes of simmering.
3. Put the salmon and 3/4 of the sauce in a zip-top bag that can be sealed.
4. Spend 30 minutes relaxing at room temperature. Spray cooking spray within the frying chamber, on the bottom and top racks, and all over the air fryer to prepare it. Set the air fryer's temperature to **390°F**.
5. Salmon should be cooked in the air fryer for 6 minutes, at a temperature of **145°F**, after being removed from the marinade.
6. Take out of the air fryer and top with a lime slice and sesame seeds. Use the leftover teriyaki sauce to serve. Enjoy!

Nutrition: calories: 298, fat: 12g, protein: 31g, carbs: 13g, fiber: 1g

48. Lemon Butter Shrimp

Ingredients

- 1 tsp. lemon juice.
- 1 tbsp. melted unsalted butter
- 1 tsp. of garlic (minced)
- 1 lb. of raw, big shrimp (peeled and deveined)
- Add pepper and salt to taste (optional) • Minced parsley (to garnish)

Prep Time: 10 min   **Cooking Time:** 10 min   **Servings:** 4

Directions

1. 4 minutes of **350°F** air fryer preheat.
2. In a sizable bowl, combine the shrimp, butter, garlic, salt, pepper, and lemon juice.
3. In the air fryer, add the shrimp mixture and cook for at least 8 minutes.
4. Add lemon wedges and parsley to garnish. Serve hot.

Nutrition: calories: 110, carbs: 1g, fat: 3.8g, protein: 18g

49. Chicken Fajitas

Ingredients

- 1 lb of skinless, boneless chicken breast
- 1 red onion (thinly sliced)
- 8 warmed tortillas
- 1/4 cup fresh coriander (chopped)
- 1 tbsp olive oil
- 1 tbsp fajita seasoning
- 1 tbsp lime juice
- 2 bell peppers (seeded and thinly sliced)

Prep Time: 15 min   **Cooking Time:** 15 min   **Servings:** 4

Directions

1. Make thin strips out of the chicken.
2. Combine the strips with the fajita seasoning, olive oil, onion, and bell pepper in a bowl. To enable coating, gently shake the dish or stir.
3. Allow to chill for at least 30 minutes or up to 5 hours.
4. Set the air fryer's temperature to **390°F** for around 5 minutes.
5. When the chicken is fully cooked and the vegetables are soft, air-fry the chicken mixture for about 15 minutes.
6. Combine the cooked chicken, cilantro, jalapeño, lime juice, and in a bowl.
7. Present with the tortillas and toppings of your choosing.

Nutrition: calories: 237, fat: 7g, protein: 32g, carbs: 4.8g, fiber: 1g

50. Lemon Garlic Shrimp

Ingredients

- 1 tbsp. olive oil
- 4 cup of small shrimp, peeled, tails removed
- 1 lemon juice and zest
- ¼ cup parsley, sliced
- 1 pinch red pepper flakes, crushed
- 4 garlic cloves, grated
- ¼ tsp. sea salt

Prep Time: 5 min   **Cooking Time:** 10 min   **Servings:** 2

Directions

1. Let air fryer heat to **400°F**.
2. Mix olive oil, lemon zest, red pepper flakes, shrimp, kosher salt, and garlic in a bowl and coat the shrimp well.
3. Place shrimps in the air fryer basket, coat with oil spray.
4. Cook at **400°F** for 8 minutes. Toss the shrimp halfway through. Serve with lemon slices and parsley.

Nutrition: calories: 140, carbs: 8g, fat: 18g, protein: 20g

51. Lemon Greek Beef and Vegetables

Ingredients

- ½ lb. (227 g.) 96% lean ground beef
- 2 medium tomatoes, chopped
- 1 onion, chopped
- 2 garlic cloves, minced
- 2 cups fresh baby spinach
- 2 tbsp. freshly squeezed lemon juice
- ⅓ cup low-sodium beef broth
- 2 tbsp. crumbled low-sodium feta cheese

Prep Time: 10 min   **Cooking Time:** 9-19 min   **Servings:** 4

Directions

1. In a baking pan, crumble the beef. Place in the air fryer basket. Air fry at **370°F** for 3 to 7 minutes, stirring once during cooking until browned.
2. Drain off any fat or liquid.
3. Swell the tomatoes, onion, and garlic into the pan. Air fry for 4 to 8 minutes more, or until the onion is tender.
4. Add the spinach, lemon juice, and beef broth.
5. Air fry for 2 to 4 minutes more, or until the spinach is wilted.
6. Sprinkle with the feta cheese and serve immediately.

Nutrition: calories: 98, fat: 1g, protein: 15g, carbs: 5g, fiber: 1g

52. Mediterranean Vegetable Skewers

Ingredients

- 2 medium-sized zucchinis, cut into 1-inch
- 2 red bell peppers,
- 1 green bell pepper, cut into 1-inch pieces
- 1 red onion, cut into 1-inch pieces
- 2 tbsp. olive oil
- Sea salt, to taste
- ½ tsp. black pepper,
- ½ tsp. red pepper flakes

Prep Time: 30 min   **Cooking Time:** 10 min   **Servings:** 4

Directions

1. Soak the skewers in water for 15 minutes.
2. Thread the vegetables on skewers; drizzle olive oil all over the vegetable skewers; sprinkle with spices.
3. Cook at **400°F** for 13 minutes.
4. Serve warm and enjoy!

Nutrition: calories: 138, carbs: 10g, fat: 10.2g, protein: 2.2g

53. Sugar Rainbow Vegetable Fritters

Ingredients

- 1 zucchini, grated and squeezed
- 1 cup corn kernels
- ½ cup canned green peas
- 2 cup. all-purpose flour
- 2 tbsp. fresh shallots, minced
- 1 tsp. fresh garlic, minced
- 1 tbsp. peanut oil Sea salt and pepper, to taste
- 1 tsp. cayenne pepper

Prep Time: 20 min   **Cooking Time:** 10 min   **Servings:** 2

Directions

1. Combine all ingredients until everything is well incorporated. Shape the mixture into patties. Spritz the Air Fryer carrier with cooking spray.
2. Cook at 365°F for 6 minutes. Fit them over and cook for a further 6 minutes
3. Serve immediately and enjoy!

Nutrition: calories: 215, fat: 8.4g, protein: 4.1g, carbs: 6g

54. Beef with Mushrooms

Ingredients

- 300 g beef
- 150 g mushrooms
- 1 onion
- 1 tsp. olive oil
- 100 g vegetable broth
- 1 tsp. basil
- 1 tsp. chili
- 30 g tomato juice

Prep Time: 15 min   **Cooking Time:** 40 min   **Servings:** 4

Directions

1. For this recipe, you should take a solid piece of beef. Take the beef and pierce the meat with a knife.
2. Rub it with olive oil, basil, and chili, and lemon juice.
3. Chop the onion and mushrooms and pour them with vegetable broth. Cook the vegetables for 5 minutes.
4. Take a big tray and put the meat in it. Add vegetable broth to the tray too. It will make the meat juicy.
5. Preheat the air fryer oven to **356°F** and cook it for 35 minutes.

Nutrition: calories: 175, carbs: 4.4g, fat: 6.2g, protein: 24.9g

55. Sugar Roasted Veggies with Yogurt

Ingredients

- 1 lb. Brussels sprouts
- 1 lb. button mushrooms
- 2 tbsp. olive oil
- ½ tsp. white pepper
- ½ tsp. dried dill weed
- ½ tsp. cayenne pepper
- ½ tsp. celery seeds
- ½ tsp. mustard seeds
- Salt, to taste

Yogurt Tahini Sauce:

- 1 cup plain yogurt
- 2 tbsp. tahini paste
- 1 tbsp. lemon juice
- 1 tbsp. olive oil
- ½ tsp. Aleppo pepper, minced

Prep Time: 20 min   **Cooking Time:** 10 min   **Servings:** 4

Directions

1. Toss the Brussels sprouts and mushrooms with olive oil and spices. Preheat your Air Fryer to **380°F**.
2. Add the Brussels sprouts to the cooking basket and cook for 10 minutes.
3. Add the mushrooms, turn the temperature to **390°F** and cook for 6 minutes more.
4. Make the sauce by whisking all ingredients.
5. Serve the warm vegetables with the sauce on the side. Bon appétit!

Nutrition: calories: 254, fat: 17.2g, protein: 8.1g, carbs: 11.1g

56. Crispy Fish Sandwiches

Ingredients

- 2 Cod fillets
- 2 tbsp. All-purpose flour
- ¼ tsp. pepper
- 1 tbsp. Lemon juice
- ¼ tsp. Salt
- ½ tsp. garlic powder
- 1 egg   ½ tbsp. mayo
- ½ cup whole wheat bread crumbs

Prep Time: 5 min   **Cooking Time:** 18 min   **Servings:** 3

Directions

1. Add salt, flour, pepper, and garlic powder to a bowl.
2. In a separate bowl, add lemon juice, mayo, and egg. In another bowl, add the breadcrumbs.
3. Coat the fish in flour, then in egg, then in breadcrumbs.
4. With cooking oil, spray the basket and put the fish in the basket. Also, spread the fish with cooking oil.
5. Cook at **400°F** for 10 minutes. This fish is soft, be careful when you flip it.

Nutrition: calories: 218, carbs: 7g, fat: 12g, protein: 22g

57. Zucchini Squash Mix

Ingredients

- 1 lb. zucchini, sliced
- 1 tbsp. parsley, chopped
- 1 yellow squash, halved, deseeded, and chopped
- 1 tbsp. olive oil
- Salt and pepper to taste

Prep Time: 10 min   **Cooking Time:** 35 min   **Servings:** 2

Directions

1. Mix all ingredients Transfer the bowl mixture into the air fryer basket and cook at **400°F** for 35 minutes.

Nutrition: calories: 49, fat: 3g, protein: 1.5g, carbs: 4g, sugar: 2g

58. Loaded Cottage Pie

Ingredients

- Large russet potatoes, peeled and halved
- 3 tbsp. extra-virgin olive oil, divided
- 1 small onion, chopped
- One handful of collard greens stemmed and thinly sliced
- 2 carrots, chopped
- 2 tomatoes, chopped
- 1 garlic clove, minced
- 1 lb. (454 g) ground beef
- ½ cup chicken broth
- 1 tsp. Worcestershire sauce
- 1 tsp. celery seeds
- 1 tsp. Smoked paprika
- ½ tsp. Dried chives
- ½ tsp. Ground mustard
- ½ tsp. cayenne pepper

Prep Time: 15 min   **Cooking Time:** 60 min   **Servings:** 6-8

Directions

1. Preheat to **400°F**.
2. Bring a large pot of water to a boil.
3. Add the potatoes and boil for 15 to 20 minutes, or until fork-tender.
4. Transfer the potatoes to a large bowl and mash with 1 tablespoon of olive oil.
5. In a cast-iron skillet, heat the remaining 2 tablespoons of olive oil.
6. Add the onion, collard greens, carrots, tomatoes, and garlic and sauté, often stirring, for 7 to 10 minutes.
7. Add the beef, broth, Worcestershire sauce, celery seeds, and smoked paprika.
8. Spread the meat and vegetable mixture evenly onto the bottom of a casserole dish. Sprinkle the chives, ground mustard, and cayenne on the mixture. Spread the mashed potatoes.
9. Transfer the casserole dish to the oven, and bake for 30 minutes, or until the top is light golden brown.

Nutrition: calories: 440, carbs: 48g, fat: 17g, protein: 27g, fiber: 9g

59. Meatballs

Ingredients

- 200 g ground beef
- 200 g ground chicken
- 100 g ground pork
- 30 g minced garlic
- 1 potato
- 1 egg
- 1 tsp. basil
- 1 tsp. cayenne pepper
- 1 tsp. white pepper
- 2 tsp. olive oil

Prep Time: 15 min   **Cooking Time:** 25 min   **Servings:** 6

Directions

1. Combine ground beef, chicken meat, and pork in the mixing bowl and stir gently.
2. Sprinkle it with basil, cayenne pepper, and white pepper.
3. Add minced garlic and egg Stir the mixture gently. You should get a fluffy mass.
4. Peel the potato and grate it.
5. Add grated potato to the mixture and stir it again.
6. Preheat the air fryer oven to **356°F**.
7. Take a tray and spray it with olive oil.
8. Make the balls from the meat mass and put them on the tray. Lay the tray in the oven and cook it for 25 minutes.

Nutrition: calories: 204, fat: 7.6g, protein: 26g, carbs: 7.1g

60. Low-Fat Steak

Ingredients

- 400 g beef steak
- 1 tsp. white pepper
- 1 tsp. turmeric
- 1 tsp. cilantro
- 1 tsp. olive oil
- 3 tsp. lemon juice
- 1 tsp. oregano
- 1 tsp. salt
- 100 g water

Prep Time: 25 min   **Cooking Time:** 10 min   **Servings:** 3

Directions

1. Rub the steaks with white pepper and turmeric and put them in the big bowl.
2. Sprinkle the meat with salt, oregano, cilantro, and lemon juice. Leave the steak for 20 minutes.
3. Combine olive oil and water and pour it into the bowl with the steaks.
4. Grill the steaks in the air fryer for 10 minutes at **265°F** from both sides. Serve it immediately.

Nutrition: calories: 268, carbs: 1.4g, fat: 10.1g, protein: 40.7g

SIDE DISHES

61. Eggplant Parmesan

Ingredients

- ½ cup and 3 tablespoons almond flour, divided
- 1.25-pound eggplant, ½-inch sliced
- 1 tbsp chopped parsley
- 1 tsp Italian seasoning
- 2 tsp salt
- 1 cup marinara sauce
- 1 egg, pastured
- 1 tbsp water
- 3 tbsp grated parmesan cheese, reduced-fat
- ¼ cup grated mozzarella cheese, reduced-fat

Prep Time: 20 min   **Cooking Time:** 15 min   **Servings:** 4

Directions

1. Slice the eggplant into ½-inch pieces, place them in a colander, sprinkle with 1 ½ teaspoon salt on both sides and let it rest for 15 minutes.
2. Meanwhile, place ½ cup flour in a bowl, add egg and water and whisk until blended.
3. Place remaining flour in a shallow dish, add remaining salt, Italian seasoning, and parmesan cheese and stir until mixed.
4. Switch on the air fryer, insert fryer basket, grease it with olive oil, then shut with its lid, set the fryer at **360°F** and preheat for 5 minutes.
5. Meanwhile, drain the eggplant pieces, pat them dry, and then dip each slice into the egg mixture and coat with flour mixture.
6. Open the fryer, add coated eggplant slices in it in a single layer, close with its lid and cook for 8 minutes until nicely golden and cooked, flipping the eggplant slices halfway through the frying.
7. Then top each eggplant slice with a tablespoon of marinara sauce and some of the mozzarella cheese and continue air frying for 1 to 2 minutes or until cheese has melted.
8. When air fryer beeps, open its lid, transfer eggplants onto a serving plate and keep them warm. Cook remaining eggplant slices in the same manner and serve.

Nutrition: calories: 193, fat: 5.5g, protein: 10g, carbs: 27g, fiber: 6g

62. Cauliflower Rice

Ingredients

For the Tofu:

- 1 cup diced carrot
- 6 ounces tofu, extra-firm, drained
- ½ cup diced white onion
- 2 tbsp soy sauce
- 1 tsp turmeric

For the Cauliflower:

- ½ cup chopped broccoli
- 3 cups cauliflower rice
- 1 tbsp minced garlic
- ½ cup frozen peas
- 1 tbsp minced ginger
- 2 tbsp soy sauce
- 1 tbsp apple cider vinegar
- 1 ½ tsp toasted sesame oil

Prep Time: 10 min   **Cooking Time:** 27 min   **Servings:** 3

Directions

1. Switch on the air fryer, insert fryer pan, grease it with olive oil, then shut with its lid, set the fryer at **370°F** and preheat for 5 minutes.
2. Meanwhile, place tofu in a bowl, crumble it, then add remaining ingredients and stir until mixed.
3. Open the fryer, add tofu mixture in it, spray with oil, close with its lid and cook for 10 minutes until nicely golden and crispy, stirring halfway through the frying.
4. Meanwhile, place all the ingredients for cauliflower in a bowl and toss until mixed.
5. When air fryer beeps, open its lid, add cauliflower mixture, shake the pan gently to mix and continue cooking for 12 minutes, shaking halfway through the frying.
6. Serve straight away.

Nutrition: calories: 258.1, fat: 13g, protein: 18.2g, carbs: 20.8g, fiber: 7g

63. Brussel Sprouts

Ingredients

- 2 cups Brussels sprouts
- ¼ tsp sea salt
- 1 tbsp olive oil
- 1 tbsp apple cider vinegar

Prep Time: 5 min   **Cooking Time:** 10 min   **Servings:** 2

Directions

1. Switch on the air fryer, insert fryer basket, grease it with olive oil, then shut with its lid, set the fryer at **400°F** and preheat for 5 minutes.
2. Meanwhile, cut the sprouts lengthwise into ¼-inch thick pieces, add them in a bowl, add remaining ingredients and toss until well coated.
3. Open the fryer, add sprouts in it, close with its lid and cook for 10 minutes until crispy and cooked, shaking halfway through the frying.
4. When air fryer beeps, open its lid, transfer sprouts onto a serving plate and serve.

Nutrition: calories: 88, fat: 4.4g, protein: 3.9g, carbs: 11g, fiber: 4g

64. Green Beans

Ingredients

- 1-pound green beans
- ¾ tsp garlic powder
- ¾ tsp ground black pepper
- 1 ¼ tsp salt
- ½ tsp paprika

Prep Time: 5 min   **Cooking Time:** 13 min   **Servings:** 4

Directions

1. Switch on the air fryer, insert fryer basket, grease it with olive oil, then shut with its lid, set the fryer at **400°F** and preheat for 5 minutes.
2. Meanwhile, place beans in a bowl, spray generously with olive oil, sprinkle with garlic powder, black pepper, salt, and paprika and toss until well coated.
3. Open the fryer, add green beans in it, close with its lid and cook for 8 minutes until nicely golden and crispy, shaking halfway through the frying.
4. When air fryer beeps, open its lid, transfer green beans onto a serving plate and serve.

Nutrition: calories: 45, carbs: 7g, fat: 1g, protein: 2g, fiber: 3g

65. Spiced Stuffed Eggplants

Ingredients

- 8 baby eggplants
- 4 tsp olive oil, divided
- ¾ tbsp dry mango powder
- ¾ tbsp ground coriander
- ½ tsp ground cumin
- ½ tsp ground turmeric
- ½ tsp garlic powder
- Salt, to taste

Prep Time: 10 min   **Cooking Time:** 12 min   **Servings:** 4

Directions

1. Preheat the Air fryer to **370°F** and grease an Air fryer basket.
2. Make slits from the bottom of each eggplant leaving the stems intact.
3. Mix one teaspoon of oil and spices in a bowl and fill each slit of eggplants with this mixture.
4. Brush each eggplant's outer side with remaining oil and arrange in the Air fryer basket.
5. Cook for about 12 minutes and dish out in a serving plate to serve hot.

Nutrition: calories: 106, fat: 3g, protein: 3g, carbs: 20g

66. Sesame Seed Bok Choy

Ingredients

- 4 hand full of baby Bok choy, bottoms removed and leaves separated
- Olive oil cooking spray
- 1 tsp garlic powder
- 1 tsp sesame seeds

Prep Time: 10 min   **Cooking Time:** 6 min   **Servings:** 4

Directions

1. Set the temperature of the air fryer to **325°F**.
2. Arrange Bok choy leaves in the air fryer basket in a single layer.
3. Spray with the cooking spray and sprinkle with garlic powder.
4. Air fry for about 5-6 minutes, shaking after every 2 minutes.
5. Remove from the air fryer and transfer the bok choy onto serving plates.
6. Garnish with sesame seeds and serve hot.

Nutrition: calories: 36, carbs: 6g, fat: 0.7g, protein: 1.5g

67. Sweet and Sour Mixed Veggies

Ingredients

- ½ lb sterling asparagus, cut into 1-½-inch pieces
- ½ lb broccoli, cut into 1-½-inch pieces
- ½ lb carrots, cut into 1-½-inch pieces
- 2 tbsp of peanut oil
- Some salt and white pepper, to taste
- ½ cup water
- 4 tbsp raisins
- 2 tbsp maple syrup
- 2 tbsp apple cider vinegar

Prep Time: 25 min   **Cooking Time:** 10 min   **Servings:** 4

Directions

1. Put the vegetables in a single layer in the lightly greased cooking basket. Drizzle the peanut oil over the vegetables.
2. Sprinkle with salt and white pepper.
3. Cook at **380°F** for 15 minutes, shaking the basket halfway through the cooking time.
4. Add ½ cup of water to a saucepan; bring it to a rapid boil, and add the raisins, maple syrup, and vinegar. Prepare for 5 to 7 minutes or until the sauce has been reduced by half.
5. Spoon the sauce over the warm vegetables and serve immediately. Bon appétit!

Nutrition: calories: 163, fat: 7.1g, protein: 3.6g, carbs: 21.6g

68. Roast Eggplant and Zucchini Bites

Ingredients

- 2 tsp fresh mint leaves, chopped
- 1-½ tsp red pepper chili flakes
- 1 pound (454 g) eggplant, peeled and cubed
- 1 pound (454 g) zucchini, peeled and cubed
- 3 tbsp olive oil

Prep Time: 35 min   **Cooking Time:** 30 min   **Servings:** 8

Directions

1. Toss all of the above ingredients in a large-sized mixing dish.
2. Roast the eggplant and zucchini bites for 30 minutes at **325°F** in your air fryer, turning once or twice.
3. Serve with a homemade dipping sauce.

Nutrition: calories: 68, carbs: 8.8g, fat: 2.5g, protein: 2.6g

69. Basil Tomatoes

Ingredients

- 2 tomatoes, halved
- Olive oil cooking spray
- Salt and ground black pepper, as required
- 1 tbsp fresh basil, chopped

Prep Time: 10 min   **Cooking Time:** 10 min   **Servings:** 2

Directions

1. Set the temperature of the air fryer to **320°F**. Grease an air fryer basket.
2. Spray the tomato halves evenly with cooking spray and sprinkle with salt, black pepper and basil.
3. Arrange tomato halves in the prepared air fryer basket, cut sides up.
4. Air fry for about 10 minutes or until they are done to your taste.
5. Remove from the air fryer and transfer the tomatoes onto serving plates.
6. Serve warm.

Nutrition: calories: 42, fat: 1.8g, protein: 1.1g, carbs: 4.8g

70. Stuffed Tomatoes

Ingredients

- 4 tomatoes
- 1 tsp olive oil
- 1 carrot, peeled and finely chopped
- 1 onion, chopped
- 1 cup frozen peas, thawed
- 1 garlic clove, minced
- 2 cups cold-cooked brown rice
- 1 tbsp soy sauce

Prep Time: 15 min   **Cooking Time:** 22 min   **Servings:** 4

Directions

1. Cut the top of each tomato and scoop out pulp and seeds.
2. In a skillet, heat oil over low heat and sauté the carrot, onion, garlic, and peas for about 2 minutes. Stir in the soy sauce and brown rice and remove from heat.
3. Set the temp of the air fryer to **355°F**. Grease an air fryer basket.
4. Stuff each tomato with the brown rice mixture.
5. Arrange tomatoes in the prepared air fryer basket.
6. Air fry for about 20 minutes.
7. Remove from the air fryer and transfer the tomatoes onto a serving platter.
8. Set aside to cool slightly. Serve warm.

Nutrition: calories: 241, carbs: 50g, fat: 1.2g, protein: 7.5g

71. Cheesy Kale

Ingredients

- ½ lb. kale
- 8 oz. parmesan cheese, shredded
- 1 onion, diced
- 1 tsp. butter
- 1 cup heavy cream

Prep Time: 10 min   **Cooking Time:** 15 min   **Servings:** 2

Directions

1. Dice up the kale, discarding any hard stems. Get a small baking dish enough to fit inside the fryer, combine the kale with the parmesan, onion, butter, and cream.
2. Pre-heat the fryer at **390°F**.
3. Set the baking dish in the fryer and cook for twelve minutes.
4. Make sure to give it a good stir before serving.

Nutrition: calories: 95, fat: 4g, protein: 5g, carbs: 12g

72. Baked Potato Topped with Cream Cheese

Ingredients

- ¼ tsp onion powder
- 1 medium russet potato, scrubbed and peeled
- 1 tbsp chives, chopped
- 1 tbsp Kalamata olives
- 1 tsp olive oil
- 1/8 tsp salt a dollop of vegan butter a dollop of vegan cream cheese

Prep Time: 10 min   **Cooking Time:** 30 min   **Servings:** 1

Directions

1. Preheat the air fryer to **400°F**.
2. Place inside the air fryer basket and cook for 30 minutes. Be sure to turn the potatoes once halfway.
3. Mash the potatoes in a mixing bowl and pour olive oil, onion powder, salt, and vegan butter.
4. Serve the potatoes with vegan cream cheese, Kalamata olives, chives, and other vegan toppings that you want.

Nutrition: calories: 145, carbs: 31g, fat: 1g, protein: 5g

73. Spices Stuffed Eggplants

Ingredients

- 8 baby eggplants
- 4 tsp olive oil, divided
- ¾ tbsp dry mango powder
- ¾ tbsp ground coriander
- ½ tsp ground cumin
- ½ tsp ground turmeric
- ½ tsp garlic powder
- Salt, to taste

Prep Time: 10 min   **Cooking Time:** 12 min   **Servings:** 4

Directions

1. Preheat the Air fryer to **370°F** and grease an Air fryer basket. Make slits from the bottom of each eggplant leaving the stems intact.
2. Mix one teaspoon of oil and spices in a bowl and fill each slit of eggplants with this mixture.
3. Brush each eggplant's outer side with remaining oil and arrange in the Air fryer basket.
4. Cook for about 12 minutes and dish out in a serving plate to serve hot.

Nutrition: calories: 106, fat: 3g, protein: 3g, carbs: 20g

74. Chickpeas and Spinach with Coconut

Ingredients

- 1 tbsp pepper
- 1 onion, chopped
- 1 tsp salt
- 4 garlic cloves, minced
- 1 can coconut milk
- 1 tbsp ginger, minced
- 1-pound spinach
- ½ cup dried tomatoes, chopped
- 1 can chickpeas
- 1 lemon, juiced
- 1 hot pepper

Prep Time: 15 min   **Cooking Time:** 20 min   **Servings:** 4

Directions

1. Preheat air fryer to **370°F**. In a bowl, mix lemon juice, tomatoes, pepper, ginger, coconut milk, garlic, salt, hot pepper, and onion. Rinse chickpeas under running water to get rid of all the gunk.
2. Put them in a large bowl. Cover with spinach.
3. Pour the sauce over and stir in oil.
4. Cook in the air fryer for 15 minutes. Serve warm.

Nutrition: calories: 124, carbs: 17g, fat: 4g, protein: 5g

75. Lemony Green Beans

Ingredients

- 1-pound green beans, trimmed and halved
- 1 tsp butter, melted
- 1 tbsp fresh lemon juice
- ¼ tsp garlic powder

Prep Time: 10 min   **Cooking Time:** 12 min   **Servings:** 3

Directions

1. Preheat the Air fryer to **400°F** and grease an Air fryer basket. Mix all the ingredients in a bowl and toss to coat well.
2. Arrange the green beans into the Air fryer basket and cook for about 12 minutes.
3. Dish out in a serving plate and serve hot.

Nutrition: calories: 60, fat: 3g, protein: 2g, carbs: 7g

76. Avocado Fries

Ingredients

- 1 medium avocado, pitted
- 1 egg ½ cup almond flour
- ¼ tsp salt
- ¼ tsp pepper
- Olive oil

Prep Time: 10 min   **Cooking Time:** 20 min   **Servings:** 2

Directions

1. Switch on the air fryer, insert the fryer basket, grease it with olive oil, then shut its lid, set the fryer at **400°F** and preheat for 10 minutes.
2. Meanwhile, cut the avocado in half and then cut each half into wedges, each about ½-inch thick.
3. Place flour in a shallow dish, add salt and black pepper and stir until mixed.
4. Crack the egg in a bowl and then whisk until blended.
5. Working on one avocado piece at a time, first dip it in egg, then coat it in almond flour mixture and place it on a wire rack.
6. Open the fryer, add avocado pieces in it in a single layer, spray oil over the avocado, close with its lid and cook for 10 minutes until nicely golden and crispy, shaking halfway through frying.
7. When the air fryer beeps, open its lid, transfer avocado fries onto a serving plate and serve.

Nutrition: calories: 251, carbs: 19g, fat: 17g, protein: 6g

77. Zucchini Fries

Ingredients

- 2 medium zucchinis
- ½ cup almond flour
- 1/8 tsp pepper
- ½ tsp garlic powder
- 1/8 tsp salt
- 1 tsp Italian seasoning
- ½ cup grated parmesan cheese
- 1 egg reduced fat, pastured, beaten
- Olive oil

Prep Time: 10 min   **Cooking Time:** 20 min   **Servings:** 4

Directions

11. Switch on the air fryer, insert the fryer basket, grease it with olive oil, then shut its lid, set the fryer at **400°F** and preheat for 10 minutes.
12. Meanwhile, cut each zucchini in half and then cut each zucchini half into 4-inch-long pieces, each about ½-inch thick.
13. Place flour in a shallow dish, add the remaining ingredients except for the egg and stir until mixed.
14. Crack the egg in a bowl and then whisk until blended.
15. Working on one zucchini piece at a time, first dip it in egg, then coat it in almond flour mixture and place it on a wire rack.
16. Open the fryer, add zucchini pieces to it a single layer, spray oil over the zucchini, close with its lid and cook for 10 minutes until nicely golden and crispy, shaking halfway through frying.
17. Cook the remaining zucchini pieces in the same manner and serve.

Nutrition: calories: 147, fat: 10g, protein: 9g, carbs: 6g

78. Radish Chips

Ingredients

- 8 oz radish slices
- ½ tsp garlic powder
- 1 tsp salt
- ½ tsp onion powder
- ½ tsp pepper

Prep Time: 5 min   **Cooking Time:** 20 min   **Servings:** 2

Directions

1. Wash radish slices, pat them dry, place them in a fryer basket, and then spray oil on them until well coated.
2. Sprinkle salt, garlic powder, onion powder, and black pepper over radish slices, and then toss until well coated.
3. Switch on the air fryer, insert the fryer basket, then shut its lid, set the fryer at **370°F**, and cook for 10 minutes, stirring slices halfway through.
4. Then spray oil on radish slices, shake the basket and continue frying for 10 minutes, stirring chips halfway through.
5. Serve straight away.

Nutrition: calories: 21, carbs: 1g, fat: 1.8g, protein: 0.2g

79. Roasted Peanut Butter Squash

Ingredients

- 1 butternut squash, peeled
- 1 tsp cinnamon
- 1 tbsp olive oil

Prep Time: 5 min   **Cooking Time:** 22 min   **Servings:** 3

Directions

1. Switch on the air fryer, insert the fryer basket, grease it with olive oil, then shut its lid, set the fryer at **220°F** and preheat for 5 minutes.
2. Meanwhile, peel squash, cut it into 1-inch pieces, and then place them in a bowl.
3. Drizzle oil over squash pieces, sprinkle with cinnamon and then toss until well coated.
4. Open the fryer, add squash pieces to it, close with its lid and cook for 17 minutes until nicely golden and crispy, shaking every 5 minutes.
5. When the air fryer beeps, open its lid, transfer squash onto a serving plate and serve.

Nutrition: calories: 179, fat: 3g, protein: 1g, carbs: 22g

80. Roasted Chickpeas

Ingredients

- 15-oz cooked chickpeas
- 1 tsp garlic powder
- 1 tbsp nutritional yeast
- 1/8 tsp cumin
- 1 tsp smoked paprika
- ½ tsp salt
- 1 tbsp olive oil

Prep Time: 35 min   **Cooking Time:** 25 min   **Servings:** 6

Directions

1. Take a large baking sheet, line it with paper towels, then spread chickpeas on it, cover peas with paper towels, and let rest for 30 minutes or until the chickpeas are dried.
2. Then switch on the air fryer, insert the fryer basket, grease it with olive oil, then shut its lid, set the fryer at **355°F**, and preheat for 5 minutes.
3. Place dried chickpeas in a bowl, add remaining ingredients and toss until well coated.
4. Add chickpeas to the fryer, close with its lid, and cook for 20 minutes until nicely golden and crispy, shaking chickpeas every 5 minutes.
5. When the air fryer beeps, open its lid, transfer chickpeas onto a serving bowl, and serve.

Nutrition: calories: 124, carbs: 17g, fat: 4.4g, protein: 4.7g

81. Buffalo Cauliflower

Ingredients

- Buffalo sauce
- ½ cup head of cauliflower, cut bite-size pieces
- 1 tbsp Olive oil
- salt & pepper, to taste

Prep Time: 5 min   **Cooking Time:** 15 min   **Servings:** 4

Directions

1. Spray cooking oil on the air fryer basket.
2. In a bowl, add buffalo sauce, pepper, and salt. Mix well. Put the cauliflower bits in the air fryer and spray the olive oil over it.
3. Let it cook at **400°F** for 7 minutes.
4. Remove the cauliflower from the air fryer and add it to the sauce.
5. Coat the cauliflower well.
6. Put the sauce coated cauliflower back into the air fryer.
7. Cook at **400°F**, for 7-8 minutes. Take out from the air fryer and serve with dipping sauce.

Nutrition: calories: 101, fat: 6.5g, protein: 3.5g, carbs: 3.7g

82. Mini Pizza

Ingredients

- Sliced olives
- 1 pita bread
- 1 tomato
- ½ cup shredded cheese

Prep Time: 2 min   **Cooking Time:** 5 min   **Servings:** 1

Directions

1. Let the air fryer preheat to **350°F**. Lay pita flat on a plate.
2. Add cheese, slices of tomatoes, and olives.
3. Cook for 5 minutes at **350°F**.

Nutrition: calories: 343.8, carbs: 36.7g, fat: 12.7g, protein: 18.5g

83. Egg Rolls

Ingredients

- Coleslaw mix: half bag
- ½ onion
- ½ tsp salt
- ½ cup of mushrooms
- 2 cup of lean ground pork
- 1 stalk of celery
- Wrappers (egg roll)

Prep Time: 10 min   **Cooking Time:** 20 min   **Servings:** 3

Directions

1. Put a skillet over medium flame, add onion and ground pork and cook for 5-7 minutes. Add mushrooms, coleslaw mixture, salt, and celery to skillet and cook for 5 minutes.
2. Lay egg roll wrapper flat and add filling (1/3 cup), roll it up, seal with water.
3. Spray with oil the rolls.
4. Put in the air fryer for 8 minutes at **400°F**, flipping once halfway through.

Nutrition: calories: 244.8, fat: 9g, protein: 11.5g, carbs: 8.5g

84. Chicken Nuggets

Ingredients

- Olive oil spray
- 2 chicken breasts, cut into bite pieces
- ½ tsp. of salt & black pepper to taste
- 2 tbsp grated parmesan cheese
- Italian seasoned breadcrumbs: 6 tbsp
- Whole wheat breadcrumbs: 2 tbsp
- 2 tsp. olive oil

Prep Time: 15 min   **Cooking Time:** 8 min   **Servings:** 4

Directions

1. Let the air fryer preheat for 8 minutes, to **400°F**.
2. In a mixing bowl, add parmesan cheese, panko, and breadcrumbs and mix well.
3. Sprinkle kosher salt, pepper, and olive oil on chicken, and mix well.
4. Take a few pieces of chicken, dunk them into breadcrumbs mixture.
5. Cook in an air fryer - sprayed with olive oil - for 8 minutes, turning halfway through.

Nutrition: calories: 188, carbs: 7.8, fat: 4.1g, protein: 25.6g

85. Chicken Tenders

Ingredients

- 4 cups chicken tenderloins
- 1 egg
- ½ cup Superfine Almond Flour
- ½ cup Powdered Parmesan cheese
- ½ tsp salt
- 1 tsp freshly ground black pepper
- ½ tsp Cajun seasoning

Prep Time: 10 min   **Cooking Time:** 15 min   **Servings:** 3

Directions

1. On a small plate, pour the beaten egg.
2. In a bowl, mix almond flour, powered Parmesan, salt, black pepper and seasoning.
3. Dip each tender in egg and then in flour mixture.
4. Using the fork to take out the tender and place it in your air fryer basket.
5. Spray the air fryer and tenders with oil spray. Cook for 12 minutes at **350°F**.
6. Raise temperature to 400°F and continue to cook for 3 minutes.

Nutrition: calories: 279.8, fat: 9.8g, protein: 20.6g, carbs: 5.4g

86. Fried Sweet Potato

Ingredients

- 1 sweet potato
- Pinch of kosher salt & freshly ground black pepper
- 1 tsp olive oil

Prep Time: 5 min   **Cooking Time:** 8 min   **Servings:** 2

Directions

1. Cut the peeled sweet potato in the shape of French fries.
2. Coat with salt, pepper, and oil.
3. Cook in the air fryer for 8 minutes, at **400°F**.
4. Cook potatoes in batches, in single layers.
5. Shake the air fryer basket once or twice. Serve with your favorite sauce.

Nutrition: calories: 59.6, carbs: 12.5g, fat: 5.4g, protein: 1.5g

87. Kale Chips

Ingredients

- 1 handful of kale
- ½ tsp. of garlic powder
- 1 tsp. of olive oil
- ½ tsp. of salt

Prep Time: 3 min   **Cooking Time:** 5 min   **Servings:** 2

Directions

1. Let the air fryer preheat to **370°F**.
2. Cut the kale into small pieces without the stem.
3. In a bowl, add all ingredients with kale pieces.
4. Add kale to the air fryer and cook for three minutes.
5. Toss it and cook for two minutes more.

Nutrition: calories: 36.9, fat: 0.9g, protein: 3.3g, carbs: 5.4g

88. Crispy Brussels Sprouts

Ingredients

- ¼ cup sliced almonds
- 2 cups Brussel sprouts
- Salt to taste
- ¼ cup grated parmesan cheese
- 2 Tbsp olive oil
- 2 Tbsp Everything bagel seasoning

Prep Time: 5 min   **Cooking Time:** 15 min   **Servings:** 4

Directions

1. In a saucepan, add Brussel sprouts with two cups of water and let it cook over medium flame for ten minutes. Drain the sprouts and cut in half.
2. In a mixing bowl, add sliced Brussel sprout with parmesan cheese, crushed almonds, oil, salt, and everything bagel seasoning. Completely coat the sprouts.
3. Cook in the air fryer for 12-15 minutes at **375°F**.

Nutrition: calories: 154.5, carbs: 2.7g, fat: 2.7g, protein: 5.8g

89. Vegetable Spring Rolls

Ingredients

- Toasted sesame seeds
- 1 large carrots – grated
- Spring roll wrappers
- 1 egg white
- Gluten-free soy sauce, a dash
- ½ cabbage: sliced
- 2 tbsp. olive oil

Prep Time: 10 min   **Cooking Time:** 15 min   **Servings:** 4

Directions

1. In a pan over high flame heat, 2 tbsp. of oil and sauté the chopped vegetables.
2. Then add soy sauce.
3. Turn off the heat and add toasted sesame seeds.
4. Lay spring roll wrappers flat on a surface and add egg white with a brush on the sides.
5. Add some vegetable mix in the wrapper and fold.
6. Spray the spring rolls with oil spray and air fry for 8 minutes at **400°F**. Serve with dipping sauce.

Nutrition: calories: 128.2, fat: 16.7g, protein: 12.4g, carbs: 7.8g

90. Zucchini Gratin

Ingredients

- 1 tbsp olive oil
- 1 tbsp chopped fresh parsley
- 2 tbsp whole wheat bread crumbs
- 1 medium zucchini
- Freshly ground black pepper & kosher salt to taste
- 4 tbsp grated parmesan cheese

Prep Time: 10 min   **Cooking Time:** 15 min   **Servings:** 4

Directions

1. Let the air fryer preheat to **375°F**. Cut zucchini in half, and a further cut in eight pieces.
2. Place in the air fryer, but do not start frying.
3. In a bowl, add cheese, parsley, black pepper, salt, bread crumbs, and oil. Mix well.
4. Add the mixture on top of the zucchini.
5. Then cook the pieces for 15 minutes.

Nutrition: calories: 80.9, carbs: 5.8g, fat: 4.9g, protein: 3.9g

GRAIN
&
BEANS

91. Veggie Quesadillas

Ingredients

- Cooking spray
- 4 whole-grain flour tortillas
- 4 oz reduced-fat sharp cheddar cheese,
- 2 tbsp chopped fresh cilantro
- 2 oz plain reduced-fat Greek yogurt
- ¼ tsp ground cumin
- ½ cup drained Pico de gallo
- 1 tsp lime zest
- 1 tbsp fresh juice (from lime)
- 1 cup sliced zucchini
- 1 cup sliced red bell pepper
- 1 cup no-salt-added canned black beans, drained and rinsed

Prep Time: 21 min   **Cooking Time:** 18 min   **Servings:** 4

Directions

1. Sprinkle 2 tbsp shredded cheese over half of each tortilla. After that, you can add cheese to the tortilla.
2. Also, add black beans, slices of zucchini, and ¼ cup of red pepper slices to the tortilla as well.
3. Remember to turn the quesadillas over after 5 minutes at **350°F**. You can air fry all quesadillas at once or in two batches.
4. While quesadillas are being cooked, mix cumin, lime juice, lime zest, and yogurt in a bowl.
5. You need to cut each of the quesadillas into wedges before you serve them. It is also necessary to sprinkle cilantro on them. Serve each of them with 1 tbsp cumin and 2 tbsp Pico de Gallo

Nutrition: calories: 291, fat: 8g, protein: 17g, carbs: 12g

92. Scrambled Tofu

Prep Time: 7 min   **Cooking Time:** 18 min   **Servings:** 2

Ingredients

- 4-6 whole wheat tortillas, warmed
- (2) 14-oz blocks of extra-firm tofu
- (1) 15-oz can of black beans, rinsed, drained
- 2 tbsp vegetable oil
- 1 onion, chopped
- ½ tsp ground cumin
- ½ tsp ground coriander
- 1 green bell pepper, chopped finely
- 1 red bell pepper, chopped finely
- 1 ½ tsp ground turmeric
- ¼ cup coarsely chopped fresh cilantro
- Salt Ground pepper

Garnishes:

- Salsa
- Scallions, sliced
- Cheddar, grated
- Avocado, chopped

Directions

1. Smash tofu using a fork or potato masher.
2. Put onion and peppers in the Air fryer basket. Cook for 2 minutes. Season with cumin and coriander. Cook for 1 minute.
3. Add in tofu. Stir in turmeric. Add beans; cook for 1 to 2 minutes at **350°F**. Stir in cilantro; season with salt and pepper.
4. Serve with tortillas and garnishes.

Nutrition: calories: 100, fat: 5g, protein: 8g, carbs: 6g

93. Potato Spread

Ingredients

- 19 oz canned garbanzo beans, dried
- 1 cup sweet potatoes, peeled and chopped
- ¼ cup tahini
- 2 tbsp lemon juice
- 1 tbsp olive oil
- 5 garlic cloves, minced
- ½ tsp cumin, ground
- 2 tbsp water
- A pinch of salt and white pepper

Prep Time: 10 min   **Cooking Time:** 10 min   **Servings:** 10

Directions

1. Put potatoes in the air fryer basket, cook them at **360°F** for 15 minutes, cool them down, peel, put them in your food processor, and pulse well.
2. Basket, add sesame paste, garlic, beans, lemon juice, cumin, water, and oil, then pulse well. Add salt and pepper, pulse again, divide into bowls and serve. Enjoy!

Nutrition: calories: 200, fat: 3g, protein: 11g, carbs: 20g

94. Mini Cheese and Bean Tacos

Ingredients

- 1 can of refried beans
- 1 oz taco seasoning mix
- 12 slices of American cheese (halved)
- 12 tortillas 1 serving of cooking spray

Prep Time: 9 min   **Cooking Time:** 23 min   **Servings:** 12

Directions

1. Place beans in a medium-sized bowl. Add seasoning mix. Combine well.
2. Place one cheese piece in the center of each tortilla. Take 1 tbsp bean mix and add it over the cheese. Add another cheese piece over the beans. Fold tortillas in half. Gently press with your hands for sealing the ends.
3. Use the cooking spray for spraying tacos.
4. Cook tacos for 3 minutes at **380°F**. Turn tacos and cook again for 3 minutes
5. Serve hot.

Nutrition: calories: 229, carbs: 20.2g, fat: 10.4g, protein: 11.3g

95. Crunchy Grains

Ingredients

- 3 cups whole grains, cooked
- ½ cup peanut oil

Prep Time: 9 min   **Cooking Time:** 16 min   **Servings:** 4

Directions

1. Use a paper towel for removing excess moisture from grains.
2. Toss grains in oil.
3. Add coated grains to the basket of the air fryer.
4. Cook for 10 minutes at **275⁰F**. Toss grains and cook again for 5 minutes.

Nutrition: calories: 71, fat: 3.2g, protein: 5.8g, carbs: 34.4g

96. Creamy Chicken, Peas, and Brown Rice

Ingredients

- 1 lb chicken breasts; cut into quarters
- 1 cup brown rice; already cooked
- 1 cup chicken stock
- ¼ cup parsley; chopped.
- 2 cups peas; frozen
- 1 ½ cups parmesan; grated
- 1 tbsp olive oil
- 3 garlic cloves; minced
- 1 yellow onion; chopped
- ½ cup white wine
- ¼ cup heavy cream
- Salt and black pepper to taste

Prep Time: 10 min   **Cooking Time:** 30 min   **Servings:** 4

Directions

1. Season chicken with salt and pepper, drizzle half of the oil over them, rub well, put in your air fryer's basket, and cook them at **360°F** for 6 minutes.
2. Preheat the pan with the rest of the oil over medium-high heat; add garlic, onion, wine, stock, salt, pepper, and heavy cream; stir and simmer. Cook for 9 minutes.
3. Transfer chicken breasts into a heat-proof dish that fits your air fryer, add peas, rice, and cream mix over them, toss, and sprinkle parmesan and parsley all over, place in your air fryer and cook at **420°F** for 10 minutes. Divide among plates and serve hot.

Nutrition: calories: 313, carbs: 27g, fat: 12g, protein: 44g

97. Jalapeño Poppers

Ingredients

- 12 to 18 whole fresh jalapeño
- 1 cup nonfat refried beans
- 1 cup shredded Monterrey jack
- 1 scallion
- 1 tsp salt, divided
- ¼ cup all-purpose flour
- 2 large eggs
- ½ cup fine cornmeal
- Olive oil or canola oil cooking spray

Directions

1. Start by slicing each jalapeño lengthwise on one side. Place jalapeños side by side in a microwave-safe bowl and microwave them until they are slightly soft, usually around 5 minutes.
2. While your jalapeños cook, mix the refried beans, scallions, ½ tsp salt, and cheese in a bowl.
3. Once your jalapeños are softened, you can scoop out the seeds and add 1 tbsp of your refried bean mixture (it can be a little less if the pepper is smaller.) Press jalapeño closed around the filling.
4. Beat eggs in a small bowl and place your flour in a separate bowl. In a third bowl, mix your cornmeal and remaining salt in a third bowl.
5. Roll each pepper in flour, then dip it in egg, and finally roll it in cornmeal, making sure to coat the entire pepper.
6. Place peppers on a flat surface and coat them with a cooking spray; olive oil cooking spray is suggested.
7. Pour into oven rack/basket. Place rack on middle-shelf of the air fryer oven. Set temperature to **400°F** and set time to 5 minutes. Select start/stop to begin. Turn each pepper, and then cook for another 5 minutes; serve hot.

Nutrition: calories: 244, fat: 12g, protein: 12g, carbs: 22g, fiber: 2.4g

98. Easy Corn and Black Bean Salsa

Ingredients

- ½ (15-oz) can of corn, drained and rinsed
- ½ (15-oz) can of black beans, drained and rinsed
- ¼ cup chunky salsa
- 2 oz reduced-fat cream cheese, softened
- ¼ cup shredded reduced-fat cheddar cheese
- ½ tsp paprika
- ½ tsp ground cumin
  Salt and freshly pepper, to taste

Prep Time: 10 min   **Cooking Time:** 10 min   **Servings:** 4

Directions

1. In a medium bowl, combine corn, black beans, cheddar cheese, cream cheese, salsa, cumin, and paprika. Sprinkle with salt and pepper and stir until well blended.
2. Pour the mixture into a baking dish.
3. Place baking dish in air fryer grill.
4. Select Air Fry, set the temperature to **325°F** and set time to 10 minutes.
5. When cooking is complete, the mixture should be heated through. Rest for 5 minutes and serve warm.

Nutrition: calories: 108, fat: 1.4g, protein: 7g, carbs: 17.4g, sugar: 2.4g

99. Quick Paella

Ingredients

- 1 (10-oz) package frozen cooked brown rice, thawed
- 1 (6-oz) jar of artichoke hearts
- ¼ cup vegetable broth
- ½ tsp turmeric
- ½ tsp dried thyme
- 1 cup frozen cooked small shrimp
- ½ cup frozen baby peas
- 1 tomato, diced

Prep Time: 7 min   **Cooking Time:** 13-17 min   **Servings:** 4

Directions

1. In a 6-by-6-by-2-inch pan, combine brown rice, artichoke hearts, vegetable broth, turmeric, and thyme, and stir gently.
2. Prepare and put in the air fryer. Cook for 9 minutes at **380°F** or until the rice is hot.
3. Remove from the air fryer and gently stir in shrimp, peas, and tomato. Cook for 5 to 8 minutes or until the shrimp and peas are hot and the paella is bubbling.

Nutrition: calories: 345, carbs: 66g, fat: 1g, protein: 18g

100. Sea Bass Paella

Ingredients

- 1 lb sea bass fillets; cubed
- 1 red bell pepper; deseeded and chopped.
- 6 scallops
- 8 shrimps, peeled and deveined
- 5 oz brown rice
- 2 oz peas
- 14 oz dry white wine
- 3 ½ oz chicken stock
- A drizzle of olive oil
- Salt and black pepper, to taste

Prep Time: 10 min   **Cooking Time:** 25 min   **Servings:** 4

Directions

1. In a heatproof dish that fits your air fryer, place all ingredients and toss.
2. Place the dish in your air fryer and cook at **380°F** for 25 minutes, stirring halfway.
3. Divide between plates and serve.

Nutrition: calories: 710, fat: 37g, protein: 51g, carbs: 68g

101. Chicken Tenders

Ingredients

- 1/8 cup almond flour
- 12 ounces chicken breasts, pastured
- ½ teaspoon ground black pepper
- ¾ teaspoon salt
- 1.2 ounces panko bread crumbs
- 1 egg white, pastured

Prep Time: 5 min   **Cooking Time:** 10 min   **Servings:** 2

Directions

1. Switch on the air fryer, insert fryer basket, grease it with olive oil, then shut with its lid, set the fryer at **350°F** and preheat for 5 minutes.
2. Meanwhile, season the chicken with salt and black pepper on both sides and then evenly coat with flour.
3. Crack the egg, whisk until blended, dip the coated chicken in it and then coat with bread crumbs.
4. Open the fryer, add chicken in it, close with its lid and cook for 10 minutes until nicely golden and cooked, turning the chicken halfway through the frying. Enjoy!

Nutrition: calories: 112, carbs: 7.1g, fat: 6.2g, protein: 7g, fiber: 0.3g

102. Chicken Nuggets

Ingredients

- 1-pound chicken breast, pastured
- 1/4 cup coconut flour
- 6 tablespoons toasted sesame seeds
- 1/2 teaspoon ginger powder
- 1/8 teaspoon sea salt
- 1 teaspoon sesame oil
- 4 egg whites, pastured

Directions

1. Switch on the air fryer, insert fryer basket, grease it with olive oil, then shut with its lid, set the fryer at **400°F** and preheat for 10 minutes.
2. Meanwhile, cut the chicken breast into 1-inch pieces, pat them dry, place the chicken pieces in a bowl, sprinkle with salt and oil and toss until well coated.
3. Place flour in a large plastic bag, add ginger and chicken, seal the bag and turn it upside down to coat the chicken with flour evenly.
4. Place egg whites in a bowl, whisk well, then add coated chicken and toss until well coated.
5. Place sesame seeds in a large plastic bag, add chicken pieces in it, seal the bag and turn it upside down to coat the chicken with sesame seeds evenly.
6. Open the fryer, add chicken nuggets in it in a single layer, spray with oil, close with its lid and cook for 12 minutes until nicely golden and cooked, turning the chicken nuggets and spraying with oil halfway through.
7. When air fryer beeps, open its lid, transfer chicken nuggets onto a serving plate and fry the remaining chicken nuggets in the same manner.
8. Serve straight away.

Nutrition: calories: 312, fat: 15g, protein: 33g, carbs: 9g, fiber: 5g

103. Chicken Meatballs

Ingredients

- 1-pound ground chicken
- 2 green onions, chopped
- ¾ tsp ground black pepper
- 1/4 cup shredded coconut, unsweetened
- 1 tsp salt
- 1 tbsp hoisin sauce
- 1 tbsp soy sauce
- 1/2 cup cilantro, chopped
- 1 tsp Sriracha sauce
- 1 tsp sesame oil

Prep Time: 5 min   **Cooking Time:** 26 min   **Servings:** 4

Directions

1. Switch on the air fryer, insert fryer basket, grease it with olive oil, then shut with its lid, set the fryer at **350°F** and preheat for 5 minutes.
2. Meanwhile, place all the ingredients in a bowl, stir until well mixed and then shape the mixture into meatballs, 1 teaspoon of chicken mixture per meatball.
3. Open the fryer, add chicken meatballs in it in a single layer, close with its lid and then spray with oil.
4. Cook the chicken meatballs for 10 minutes, flipping the meatballs halfway through, and then continue cooking for 3 minutes until golden.
5. When air fryer beeps, open its lid, transfer chicken meatballs onto a serving plate and then cook the remaining meatballs in the same manner.
6. Serve straight away.

Nutrition: calories: 223, fat: 14g, protein: 20g, carbs: 3g, fiber: 1g

104. Buffalo Chicken Hot Wings

Ingredients

- 16 chicken wings, pastured
- 1 tsp garlic powder
- 2 tsp chicken seasoning
- ¾ teaspoon ground black pepper
- 2 tsp soy sauce
- 1/4 cup buffalo sauce, reduced-fat

Prep Time: 10 min   **Cooking Time:** 45 min   **Servings:** 6

Directions

1. Switch on the air fryer, insert fryer basket, grease it with olive oil, then shut with its lid, set the fryer at **400°F** and preheat for 5 minutes.
2. Meanwhile, place chicken wings in a bowl, drizzle with soy sauce, toss until well coated and then season with black pepper and garlic powder.
3. Open the fryer, stack chicken wings in it, then spray with oil and close with its lid.
4. Cook the chicken wings for 10 minutes, turning the wings halfway through, and then transfer them to a bowl, covering the bowl with a foil to keep the chicken wings warm.
5. Air fry the remaining chicken wings in the same manner, then transfer them to the bowl, add buffalo sauce and toss until well coated.
6. Return chicken wings into the fryer basket in a single layer and continue frying for 7 to 12 minutes or until chicken wings are glazed and crispy, shaking the chicken wings every 3 to 4 minutes.
7. Serve straight away.

Nutrition: calories: 88, fat: 6.5g, protein: 4.5g, carbs: 2.6g

105. Herb Chicken Thighs

Ingredients

- 6 chicken thighs, skin-on, pastured
- 2 tsp garlic powder
- 1/2 tsp onion powder
- 1 tsp dried basil
- 1 tsp spike seasoning
- 1/2 tsp dried sage
- 1/4 tsp ground black pepper
- 1/2 tsp dried oregano
- 2 tbsp lemon juice
- 1/4 cup olive oil

Prep Time: 6 h 25 min   **Cooking Time:** 40 min   **Servings:** 6

Directions

1. Prepare the marinade and for this, place all the ingredients in a bowl, except for chicken, stir until well combined and then pour the marinade in a large plastic bag.
2. Add chicken thighs in the plastic bag, seal the bag, then turn in upside down until chicken thighs are coated with the marinade and let marinate in the refrigerator for minimum of 6 hours.
3. Then drain the chicken, arrange the chicken thighs on a wire rack and let them rest for 15 minutes at room temperature.
4. Meanwhile, switch on the air fryer, insert fryer basket, grease it with olive oil, then shut with its lid, set the fryer at **360°F** and preheat for 5 minutes.
5. Then open the fryer, add chicken thighs in it in a single layer top-side down, close with its lid, cook the chicken for 8 minutes, turn the chicken, and continue frying for 6 minutes.
6. Turn the chicken thighs and then continue cooking for another 6 minutes or until chicken is nicely browned and cooked.
7. When air fryer beeps, open its lid, transfer chicken onto a serving plate and cook the remaining chicken thighs in the same manner. Serve straight away.

Nutrition: calories: 163, fat: 9.2g, protein: 19.4g, carbs: 1g, fiber: 0.3g

106. Chicken Wings

Ingredients

- 6 Chicken wings - Flats and drumettes
- Olive oil spray
- Salt Pepper
- Sauce of your choice

Prep Time: 5 min   **Cooking Time:** 15 min   **Servings:** 4

Directions

1. Spray the air fryer basket or foil-lined air fryer basket with non-stick cooking spray.
2. Arrange the wings equally in the basket.
3. Coat with an even layer of olive oil spray, and add a pinch of salt and pepper to the wings.
4. Pre-heat to **390°F** for 10 minutes.
5. Turn and cook for an additional 10 minutes.
6. Using a thermometer, check that the temperature of the wings is at least **165°F**.
7. Coat with sauce if you prefer, or other dipping sauces.

Nutrition: calories: 136, fat: 9.1g, protein: 12.7g, carbs: 1.8g

107. Spicy Chicken Meatballs

Ingredients

- 1 medium red onion, minced
- 2 garlic cloves, minced
- 1 jalapeño pepper, minced
- 2 tsp olive oil
- 3 tbsp ground almonds
- 1 egg 1 tsp dried thyme
- 1 pound of ground chicken breast

Prep Time: 10 min   **Cooking Time:** 11-14 min   **Servings:** 24

Directions

1. In a pan, combine the red onion, garlic, jalapeño, and olive oil. Bake for 3 to 4 minutes in the air fryer, or until the vegetables are crisp but tender. Transfer to a medium bowl.
2. Mix the almonds, egg and thyme into the vegetable mixture. Add the chicken and mix until just combined.
3. Form the chicken mixture into about 24 (1-inch) balls. Bake the meatballs, in batches, for 8 to 10 minutes, until the chicken reaches an internal temperature of **165°F** on a meat thermometer.

Nutrition: calories: 40, carbs: 0.3g, fat: 5.2g, protein: 5.2g

108. Salted Biscuit Pie Turkey Chops

Ingredients

- 8 large turkey chops
- 300g crackers
- 2 eggs
- ½ tsp extra virgin olive oil
- Salt to taste
- Ground pepper to taste

Prep Time: 5 min   **Cooking Time:** 20 min   **Servings:** 4

Directions

1. Put the turkey chops on the worksurface and add salt and pepper. Beat the eggs in a bowl.
2. Crush the cookies with a blender and then place them in a bowl. Coat the chops with the beaten eggs followed by the crushed cookies. Press well so that the empanada is perfect.
3. Brush the empanada with olive oil, using a silicone brush. Put the chops in the basket of the air fryer, in batches.
4. Cook in the air fryer at **400°F** for 15 minutes.
5. When you have made them all, serve.

Nutrition: calories: 259, fat: 7.6g, protein: 31.3g, carbs: 12.4g

109. Chicken Wings

Ingredients

- 10 chicken wings (about 700 g) Oil spray
- 1 tbsp soy sauce
- ½ tbsp cornstarch
- 2 tbsp maple syrup
- 1 tbsp ground fresh chili paste
- 1 tbsp minced garlic
- ½ tsp chopped fresh ginger
- 1 tbsp lime sumo
- ½ tbsp salt
- 2 tbsp chives

Prep Time: 10 min   **Cooking Time:** 25 min   **Servings:** 2

Directions

1. Pat the chicken dry with a tea towel. Cover the chicken with the oil spray.
2. Place the chicken wings inside the air fryer, making sure that they do not overlap each other.
3. Cook at **400°F** until the skin is crispy. This should take about 25 minutes. Turn them at the half way point.
4. Mix the soy sauce with cornstarch in a small pan. Add maple syrup, chili paste, garlic, ginger, and lime sumo.
5. Simmer until it boils and thickens.
6. Put chicken in a bowl, add the sauce and cover all the chicken. Sprinkle with chives.

Nutrition: calories: 451, carbs: 14.5g, fat: 26.4g, protein: 37.4g

110. Mini Turkey Meatballs

Ingredients

- 3 tbsp olive oil
- 3 tbsp ketchup
- 3 garlic cloves, minced
- ¼ tsp ground black pepper
- ¼ cup grated Pecorino Romano
- ¼ cup grated Parmesan
- ¼ cup dried breadcrumbs
- ¼ cup Italian parsley leaves, chopped
- 1 tsp salt 1 small onion, grated
- 1 pound of ground dark turkey meat
- 1 large egg

Prep Time: 15 min   **Cooking Time:** 10 min   **Servings:** 5

Directions

1. Get a big bowl. Add pepper, salt, Pecorino, Parmesan, parsley, ketchup, breadcrumbs, egg, garlic, and onion. Mix them together.
2. Whisk them until they mix evenly. Add the turkey and mix.
3. Shape the mixture into several meatballs. Air fry the meatballs for about 5 minutes at **380°F** until they are brown.
4. Add your meatballs to your favorite sauce.
5. You can now serve the turkey meatballs. They are best served either warm or hot.

Nutrition: calories: 261, fat: 13.6g, protein: 25.6g, carbs: 9.1g

EXTRA. Turkey Breast

Ingredients

- 4 pound of turkey breast, with the rib removed
- 2 tsp of kosher salt
- 1/2 tbsp of dry turkey or poultry seasoning
- 1 tbsp of olive oil

Prep Time: 20 min   **Cooking Time:** 35 min   **Servings:** 4

Directions

6. Coat the turkey breast with ½ tablespoon of oil.
7. The next step is to season both sides of the turkey breast with salt and turkey seasoning. You can add the remaining oil to the seasoned turkey.
8. Preheat your air fryer to **350°F** before cooking the turkey for 20 minutes.
9. Turn it over and cook it at **160°F** for another 30 to 35 minutes.
10. Let it cool for 10 minutes before you carve it.

Nutrition: calories: 226, carbs: 0.3g, fat: 10g, protein: 32.5g

EXTRA. Turkey and Cream Cheese Breast Pillows

Ingredients

- 1 cup of milk with
- 1 egg inside (put the egg in the cup and then fill with milk)
- 1/3 cup of water
- 1/4 cup olive oil or oil
- 1-3/4 tsp of salt
- 2 tbsp trivia sweetener
- 2-1/2 tbsp dried granular yeast
- 4 cups of flour
- 1 egg yolk to brush
- 2 jars of cream cheese
- 15 slices of turkey breast cut in 4

Prep Time: 5 min   **Cooking Time:** 10 min   **Servings:** 4

Directions

1. Mix all the dough ingredients with your hands until it is very smooth.
2. After the ready dough, make small balls and place on a floured surface.
3. Open each dough ball with a roller trying to make it square.
4. Cut squares of approximately 4x4 in.
5. Fill with a piece of turkey breast and 1 teaspoon of cream cheese coffee. Close the union of the masses joining the 4 points.
6. Brush with the egg yolk and set aside.
7. Preheat the air fryer. Set the timer of 5 minutes and the temperature to **392°F**.
8. Place 6 units in the air fryer's basket and bake for 4 or 5 minutes at **356°F**.
9. Repeat until all the pillows have finished cooking.

Nutrition: calories: 538, fat: 29.97g, protein: 43.64g, carbs: 22.7g

COOKING CONVERSION CHART

MEASUREMENT

CUP	ONCES	MILLILITERS	TABLESPOONS
8 cup	64 oz	1895 ml	128
6 cup	48 oz	1420 ml	96
5 cup	40 oz	1180 ml	80
4 cup	32 oz	960 ml	64
2 cup	16 oz	480 ml	32
1 cup	8 oz	240 ml	16
3/4 cup	6 oz	177 ml	12
2/3 cup	5 oz	158 ml	11
1/2 cup	4 oz	118 ml	8
3/8 cup	3 oz	90 ml	6
1/3 cup	2.5 oz	79 ml	5.5
1/4 cup	2 oz	59 ml	4
1/8 cup	1 oz	30 ml	3
1/16 cup	1/2 oz	15 ml	1

WEIGHT

IMPERIAL	METRIC
1/2 oz	15 g
1 oz	29 g
2 oz	57 g
3 oz	85 g
4 oz	113 g
5 oz	141 g
6 oz	170 g
8 oz	227 g
10 oz	283 g
12 oz	340 g
13 oz	369 g
14 oz	397 g
15 oz	425 g
1 lb	453 g

TEMPERATURE

FAHRENHEIT	CELSIUS
100 °F	37 °C
150 °F	65 °C
200 °F	93 °C
250 °F	121 °C
300 °F	150 °C
325 °F	160 °C
350 °F	180 °C
375 °F	190 °C
400 °F	200 °C
425 °F	220 °C
450 °F	230 °C
500 °F	260 °C
525 °F	274 °C
550 °F	288 °C

Printed in Great Britain
by Amazon